The People's Bible Teachings

# GOD'S PROVIDENCE

## He Cares for You

Mark J. Lenz

NORTHWESTERN PUBLISHING HOUSE
Milwaukee, Wisconsin

Library of Congress Card 96-71377
Northwestern Publishing House
1250 N. 113th St., Milwaukee, WI 53226-3284
© 1997 by Northwestern Publishing House.
Published 1997
Printed in the United States of America
ISBN 0-8100-0673-1

# Table of Contents

# Editor's Preface

The People's Bible Teachings is a series of books on all of the main doctrinal teachings of the Bible.

Following the pattern set by The People's Bible series, these books are written especially for laypeople. Theological terms, when used, are explained in everyday language so that people can understand them. The authors show how Christian doctrine is drawn directly from clear passages of Scripture and then how those doctrines apply to people's faith and life. Most importantly, these books show how every teaching of Scripture points to Christ, our only Savior.

The authors of The People's Bible Teachings are parish pastors and professors who have had years of experience teaching the Bible. They are men of scholarship and practical insight.

We take this opportunity to express our gratitude to Professor Leroy Dobberstein of Wisconsin Lutheran Seminary, Mequon, Wisconsin, and Professor Thomas Nass of Martin Luther College, New Ulm, Minnesota, for serving as consultants for this series. Their insights and assistance have been invaluable.

We pray that the Lord will use these volumes to help his people grow in their faith, knowledge, and understanding of his saving teachings, which he has revealed to us in the Bible. To God alone be the glory.

Curtis A. Jahn
Series Editor

# Introduction

No matter how hard you try, you just can't seem to remember that day. You're totally dependent on other people to tell you about it. You know that your parents were there. Even both sets of grandparents were there. Not all your aunts and uncles were able to make it, but a couple of them did. Quite a number of other people were there too, and they were all interested in you. All these people were concerned about you. They were praying for you. But they didn't know you very well because you were only 12 days old.

Your pastor was there too. He was the one who poured water on your head and said, "I baptize you in the name of the Father and of the Son and of the Holy Spirit." He spoke words of Scripture and prayer, and then toward the end of the ceremony he spoke these words: "The LORD will watch over your coming and going both now and forevermore" (Psalm 121:8). Depending on how long ago that day was, your pastor may have spoken those words in the King James Version: "The LORD shall preserve thy going out and thy coming in from this time forth, and even for evermore." He spoke those words because they are part of the traditional Baptism liturgy.

Your baptism was the day when you entered the kingdom of God. By the washing of water and the Word, the guilt of all your sins was washed away, all the benefits of Christ's sacrifice were applied to you, and your heavenly Father established an eternal covenant with you, assuring you that he is your dear Father and that you are his dear child . . . forever. Baptism is your guarantee that your

Father in heaven loves you so much that he is going to care for you all the days of your life and then take you to be with him in the mansions of heaven above.

The psalm from which those words of the Baptism liturgy are taken is one of the psalms of ascent. People sang these psalms while they ascended the hills leading up to Jerusalem or while they ascended the steps leading up to the temple in Jerusalem. As they climbed the hills toward Jerusalem and saw other hills in the distance, they were reminded that their help came "from the LORD, the Maker of heaven and earth" (Psalm 121:2). These believers of the Old Testament knew that the Lord would not let their feet slip as they walked up the hills or as they walked up the steps. He would watch over them all the time—day and night—because he never sleeps.

One night four-year-old Sarah didn't want to go to bed because she was afraid of the dark. Her mother tried to soothe her, but Sarah wouldn't go to bed unless her mother was right there with her. When her mother finally turned off the lights, Sarah saw the moon outside her window. "Mommy," she asked, "will God put out his light and go to sleep now too?" "No," her mother said, "God never goes to sleep." "Well," Sarah said, "if God isn't going to go to sleep, there's no sense in both of us staying awake, is there?" Because God is your heavenly Father, you know that he stays awake to watch over not just four-year-old girls but also you and all his people.

As you read further in Psalm 121, you learn that the Lord who never sleeps "will keep you from all harm" when you're sleeping or at any time (verse 7). You remember the time when you built a snow fort for protection from snow-balls and hard-packed iceballs that could really hurt. You had built that fort in the school playground after a particularly heavy snowfall, and every recess for a couple of days you remember choosing up sides and having snowball fights. That snow fort protected you. It kept you from getting seriously hurt. That's the picture here of how God protects you from all harm. He builds a fort around you to protect you.

You think back to all the many ways God has protected you throughout your life. You think about the thousands of miles you've traveled by car and airplane. You think about all the miles you put on your bicycle when you were young. Your life was spared. You were protected from harm. The Lord was there to "build a fort" around you. You think about the time you narrowly missed being hit by a train as you were driving through an unguarded railroad crossing. You could have been killed. But the Lord was there to build a fort around you. You think about how the Lord protected you on vacation trips, how one morning you found huge bear paw prints on the plastic outside your tent just inches from where your face had been during the night. You remember how, on another occasion, a ferocious storm caused your tent to blow down with you and your family inside, but you were spared. You remember how as a youngster you fell through a hole in the floor of an old fort you were visiting with your parents but somehow came out of it completely uninjured. The Lord was there to build a fort around you.

The Lord will "watch over your life," Psalm 121 continues (verse 7). The Hebrew word translated as "life" could be translated as "breathing," but it could also be translated as "soul." The Lord will watch over your soul. You think about how the Lord has been taking care of your spiritual life ever since you were baptized. He was watching over your soul as your parents taught you about Jesus and prayer. He was watching over your soul when, as a child of four years, you went to vacation Bible school for the first time. You only lasted a day before homesickness forced you to drop out, but the Lord was watching over you then too. You think about how the Lord watched over your soul through your Sunday school teachers, eight years of Lutheran elementary school, and confirmation instruction. Through all your teachers and the lessons they taught, the Lord was watching over your soul. The Lord was there when you were confirmed, and he was concerned about the next door you would enter in your spiritual life. The Lord nourished and strengthened the faith he had planted in your heart during the years you spent at a Lutheran high school. By means of Christian teachers, in a Christian environment, and with Christian friends, the Lord was watching over your soul. The Lord has been there watching over your soul every time you entered church to hear his Word, every time you approached the altar to receive the Sacrament of Holy Communion.

"The LORD will watch over your coming and going," Psalm 121 continues (verse 8). The Lord has watched over you to this point in your life, and he promises to care for you for the rest of your life. Each day as you go to work, the Lord watches over you. Throughout the day he watches over you. When you come home from work, he watches over you. Every time you enter your car and drive the streets and freeways, the Lord is watching over you. Wherever you go and whatever you do, the Lord is watching over your coming and going.

As you read further in verse 8, you realize that it obviously has a wider application because it says, "The LORD will watch over your coming and going both now and forevermore." You realize that because you are his dear child, the Lord will watch over your life no matter where you go, no matter what you do, and no matter how long you live. And, finally, he will watch over you when you exit this life by sending his angels to take your soul to heaven, where you will live under his eternal protection, where you will enjoy everlasting safety and security. Just as you were kept safe and secure when you entered this life, so you will be kept safe when you exit this life. That's how much God cares for you.

You realize, of course, that your life has not been, nor will it ever be, free from troubles, sorrows, and problems. You've had your share of those. But you've come to understand that "we must go through many hardships to enter the kingdom of God" (Acts 14:22), and you realize that when those hardships come, you have the Lord's assurance that "he will also provide a way out so that you can stand up under" them (1 Corinthians 10:13). God doesn't promise you a trouble-free life, but he does promise that when troubles come, he will care for you. He will give you the strength to deal with those troubles; he will lead you safely through them; he will show you the way out; and eventually he will take you to himself, where you will never again experience troubles of any kind.

The work of God we have been describing is called the providence of God. God preserves and protects us. This is the topic we will consider in this book. It is a topic of great importance and value because it offers us splendid comfort. As we learn what the Bible teaches about God's providence, may it lead us to thank and praise the Lord for this great work he is doing for us every moment of our lives.

# 1

# The Nature of God's Providence

You wonder what else can go wrong. You had to cancel the trip because of the storm. For weeks the entire family had been looking forward to going to Grandma's house. It won't even seem like Thanksgiving without the delicious feast you've come to expect. There's little food in the house. No one can come to visit you because traveling is too treacherous. Here you are, all alone, shut in with nothing to do.

### God provides for you

Feeling sorry for yourself, you pick up your Bible and start paging through the book of Job. As you read, you begin to realize that you're like Job in a way you hadn't expected. You read the Lord's words to Job: "Where were you [Job] when I laid the earth's foundation? Tell me, if you understand" (38:4). "Have you ever given orders to the morning, or shown the dawn its place, that it might take the earth by the edges and shake the wicked out of it?" (verses 12,13). "Have you entered the storehouses of the snow or seen the storehouses of the hail . . . ?" (verse 22). "From whose womb comes the ice? Who gives birth to the frost from the heavens when the waters become hard as stone, when the surface of the deep is frozen?" (verses 29,30).

You realize the Lord could be speaking to you instead of Job. As you read on, you hear the Lord ask Job if he can put the stars in the sky, if he knows the laws of the heavens, if he can make it rain, if he can provide food for lions and ravens. The list goes on. The Lord tells Job that he provides for mountain goats, deer, donkeys, wild oxen, ostriches, horses, hawks, etc. You think, yes, the Lord is in control of everything. The Lord provides—not me! Who do I think I am?

The Bible contains many examples of how God provides for his people. The Lord caused the waters of the Red Sea to separate so that the Israelites could go across on dry land. He drowned the armies of Pharaoh in the Red Sea. He provided water, manna, and quail for his people in the wilderness.

In Moses' farewell address to the people of Israel shortly before they entered the Promised Land, he said: "The LORD your God has blessed you in all the work of your hands. He has watched over your journey through this vast desert. These forty years the LORD your God has been with you, and you have not lacked anything" (Deuteronomy 2:7).

The Israelites did not lack anything for 40 years! The Lord still provides for his people today, although not usually in such a dramatic way. Being able to buy bread from a supermarket and having water instantly available by turn- ing on a faucet doesn't seem as dramatic as manna from heaven and water from a rock, but the Lord is providing just the same.

The story about the prophet Elijah being fed by ravens comes to mind. Nothing can keep the Lord from providing for his people, not even drought and famine. Being brought bread and meat by ravens is a remarkable way to have one's needs provided for, but it's no more remarkable than refrigerators and freezers in which we store our food and ovens and microwaves in which we prepare it.

When the brook where Elijah had been staying dried up, the Lord told him to go to Zarephath, where a widow would supply him with food. At the town gate of Zarephath a widow was gathering sticks. Elijah called to her and asked, "Would you bring me a little water in a jar so I may have a drink?" (1 Kings 17:10). As she went to get it, he called to her also to bring him a piece of bread. She replied, "I don't have any bread—only a handful of flour in a jar and a little oil in a jug. I am gathering a few sticks to take home and make a meal for myself and my son, that we may eat it—and die" (verse 12). Elijah told her to go and make a small cake of bread for him first and then make something for herself and her son because the Lord had promised that the jar of flour would not be used up and the jug of oil would not run dry until the Lord gave rain to the land once again. So it happened. The jar of flour was not used up, and the jug of oil did not run dry. The home of the widow of Zarephath became a place of plenty—just as the country in which we live is a land of plenty.

Zarephath wasn't the last place the Lord provided in plentiful fashion for his prophet Elijah. After his confrontation with the prophets of Baal at Mount Carmel, Elijah had to flee for his life because wicked Queen Jezebel was trying to kill him. Alone in the desert Elijah decided he had had enough. He prayed that he might die. "Then he lay down under the tree and fell asleep. All at once an angel touched him and said, 'Get up and eat.' He looked around, and there by his head was a cake of bread baked over hot coals, and a jar of water" (1 Kings 19:5,6). This all happened a second time. Strengthened by the food, Elijah continued on his journey to Mount Horeb.

There's nothing like a good meal to renew one's zest for living and one's determination to keep going. You marvel at how the Lord has provided you with three meals a day for your entire life! Maybe you'll miss Grandma's Thanksgiving feast, but you'll eat very well anyway.

You recall how Elijah's successor, Elisha, was the Lord's instrument to provide for people. Once the widow of one of the prophets came in desperation to Elisha to tell him that her husband's creditor was coming to take her two boys as slaves. Elisha told her to go around to all her neighbors and collect empty jars. She was to ask for all they had. She was not to be satisfied with just a few. Then she was to go into her home and pour oil into the jars and, as each one was filled, to put it aside. The oil did not cease coming until all the jars she had borrowed were filled! Elisha told her to sell the oil so she could pay her debts, and she and her sons could live on what was left (2 Kings 4:1-7).

You think about the times when you wondered how you would pay the bills. When the children were little and there wasn't as much income as there is now, you used to wonder sometimes if there would be enough to buy groceries. But somehow there was always enough. The Lord always provided—sometimes more plentifully than you could ever have imagined!

You begin to realize that the Scriptures are filled with examples of how the Lord provides. Psalm 23 assures you that because the Lord is your shepherd, you will not "be in want" (verse 1). As a shepherd brings his sheep and lambs to green pastures and leads them "beside quiet waters" (verse 2), so he gives you all you need every day. But not only what you need. Often he provides even more than you need. Your "cup overflows" (verse 5). The prophet Joel says, "Be glad, O people of Zion, rejoice in the LORD your God. . . . He sends you abundant showers, both autumn and spring rains. . . . The threshing floors will be filled with grain; the vats will overflow with new wine and oil" (2:23,24).

The Lord doesn't just provide. He provides plenty. And sometimes he provides to a superabundant degree! To those who had robbed God by withholding their tithes and offerings, the Lord through his prophet Malachi said, "'Bring the whole tithe into the storehouse, that there may be food in my house. Test me in this,' says the LORD Almighty, 'and see if I will not throw open the floodgates of heaven and pour out so much blessing that you will not have room enough for it'" (3:10).

Why does the Lord provide? Why does he sometimes provide much more than you need? Surely it's an example of his amazing love. But when he showers you with blessings, does he not also do it so that you might learn to use them wisely, to his glory and for the welfare of others? So that you might take from your abundance to help those who are less fortunate? So that you might save and invest for a rainy day?

### God protects you

You look outside and notice that the wind has started to pick up. The snow is coming sideways, and the drifts are piling high. It wouldn't be any fun to be on the highways. You're cozy and warm, and your family is safe inside your well-insulated home with its efficient furnace. The Lord is protecting and sheltering you from the storm that rages outside.

It wasn't a blizzard from which David needed protection, but "men whose teeth are spears and arrows, whose tongues are sharp swords" (Psalm 57:4). As he fled from jealous King Saul, who was determined to kill him, David took refuge in a cave. But the cave was only the outward means of David's protection. David said, "Have mercy on me, O God, . . . for in you my soul takes refuge. I will take refuge in the shadow of your wings until the disaster has passed" (verse 1).

You can't see him, but according to his promise you know he is protecting you from that blizzard raging outside. You realize what wonderful and amazing things you would behold if your eyes could be opened to see God and his holy angels all around you. Once, the Arameans attacked the kingdom of Israel. Their army had surrounded the capital city of Samaria with its horses and chariots. When the servant of the prophet Elisha saw the city surrounded, he asked Elisha, "Oh, my lord, what shall we do?" The prophet answered, "'Don't be afraid. . . . Those who are with us are more than those who are with them.' And Elisha prayed, 'O LORD, open his eyes so he may see'" (2 Kings 6:15-17). Then the Lord opened the servant's eyes so he could see the hills full of horses and chariots of fire all around Elisha.

You don't see the angels, but you realize that God regularly sends them to protect you and your family even as he protected Daniel in the lions' den. Spurred by his wicked administrators who were jealous of Daniel, the Persian king Darius had decreed that anyone who prayed to any god or man except to him would be thrown into the lions' den. When Daniel continued his daily habit of praying to the Lord, he was thrown into the lions' den. Early in the morning when Darius came to the den to see if Daniel had survived, Daniel answered his anxious concerns by saying, "My God sent his angel, and he shut the mouths of the lions. They have not hurt me, because I was found inno-cent in his sight" (Daniel 6:22).

How frequently the writers of Scripture speak about God's protection. "You have been a refuge for the poor," prays the prophet Isaiah, "a refuge for the needy in his dis-tress, a shelter from the storm" (25:4). The Lord is shelter-ing you from the storm right now. The Lord is covering you with the shadow of his hand (Isaiah 51:16) even as he protected his Old Testament people. The angel of the Lord is encamping around you (Psalm 34:7). The Lord is covering you with his feathers, and under his wings you find refuge; his faithfulness is your shield and rampart (Psalm 91:4). "As the mountains surround Jerusalem," so the Lord is surrounding you "both now and forevermore" (Psalm 125:2).

### Protection promised to believers

God's protection is a special promise given to believers. Esau held a grudge against his brother, Jacob, because of the blessing their father had given to Jacob. Esau was even determined to kill his brother. As he fled for his life, Jacob stopped at Bethel for the night and used a stone for his pillow. He had a dream in which he heard the Lord say to him, "All peoples on earth will be blessed through you and your offspring. I am with you and will watch over you wherever you go, and I will bring you back to this land" (Genesis 28:14,15). Together with the promise of the Savior from sin, the Lord also assured Jacob of protection. And so it happened. After many years in Haran, years filled with difficulties and troubles, the Lord brought Jacob safely back to the land of promise.

You think of the many places to which you have traveled over the years and realize how often the Lord has brought you safely back home. It's another example of the Father's love for you.

On the night before his crucifixion Jesus prayed for his disciples, "I will remain in the world no longer, but they [the disciples] are still in the world, and I am coming to you. Holy Father, protect them by the power of your name" (John 17:11). That was Jesus' prayer for the disciples, and that is his prayer for you, one of his modern-day disciples. The Father has all power in heaven and earth, and by that power he promises to protect you. Yes, God has power to do what he promises (Romans 4:21).

### Infinite care

But, you think, does God really have time to be concerned about the little details in my life? He has the heavens and earth to watch over, the entire universe to protect. Can he really concern himself with my family's trips to Grandma's house and our protection from the blizzard?

In his Sermon on the Mount Jesus says that God is concerned about wild flowers and grass in the fields and sparrows in the heavens, in other words, about every little thing in the world. "So do not worry, saying, 'What shall we eat?' or 'What shall we drink?' or 'What shall we wear?' For the pagans run after all these things, and your heavenly

Father knows that you need them" (Matthew 6:31,32). "Indeed, the very hairs of your head are all numbered" (Luke 12:7). With wonderful promises like that, what cause for worry could we ever have? You begin to have a fresh understanding of Peter's encouragement to "cast all your anxiety on him because he cares for you" (1 Peter 5:7).

You look up from your reading and notice the print of Jesus, the Good Shepherd, hanging on your living room wall. Surrounded by sheep and lambs, he is holding a little lamb in his arms. Of all the pictures depicting God's providence painted for us in Scripture, this has to be one of the most beautiful. You think about the 23rd psalm.

"The LORD is my shepherd, I shall not be in want" (verse 1). I shall never be in want because the Lord will always be there to take care of me. "He makes me lie down in green pastures" (verse 2). I can lie down on my bed at night and go to sleep with the peaceful assurance that the Lord is watching over me. During the day he provides me with all I need for my body and life. "He leads me beside quiet waters" (verse 2). You think about how quiet and calm the lake was one early morning at the cabin last summer. What a picture of peace! And just as a shepherd leads the sheep and lambs to drink, so the Lord, the Good Shepherd, refreshes you with food and drink for your body and nourishment for your soul. "He restores my soul," David says (verse 3).

"Even though I walk through the valley of the shadow of death, I will fear no evil, for you are with me; your rod and your staff, they comfort me" (verse 4). The blizzard raging outside is by no means the darkest valley you could go through. There could be many worse things. There could be a tornado, hurricane, earthquake, volcanic eruption. There could be war in your country or anarchy and fighting in the streets. But regardless of what could happen, you have no reason to fear because the Lord, your Good Shepherd, is with you. He will protect you from all harm and danger. He will watch over your life and keep you safe. What comfort you can take in that assurance.

You look at that picture again. Did the artist have the 23rd psalm in mind? Perhaps. But you begin to wonder if he maybe was thinking of a verse in Isaiah: "He tends his flock like a shepherd: He gathers the lambs in his arms and carries them close to his heart; he gently leads those that have young" (40:11). You picture yourself and your family as the sheep and the lambs in that painting. The Good Shepherd is concerned about each of you. No problem or need ever escapes his notice. That's your little infant daughter he has in his arms close to his heart. You love your children and want to do all you can to protect them and provide for them, but how relieved you are to know that it is actually the Good Shepherd who is doing that.

That Good Shepherd, of course, is Jesus. That's how he wants you to think of him. You turn to the tenth chapter of John where you hear Jesus say, "I am the good shepherd. The good shepherd lays down his life for the sheep" (verse 11). He is not just a shepherd, not even just a good shepherd, but a shepherd who laid down his life for the sheep. If he took care of your greatest need, paying the price of your redemption, will he not also take care of all your daily, earthly needs as well?

### God supports the weak

You're beginning to feel the effects of shoveling that wet, heavy snow a couple hours ago. You gave up because it was piling up faster than you could shovel it. You can feel a nap coming on. It's a good thing your family's continuing welfare doesn't depend totally on you. Sometimes you feel so tired. Right now you feel as though your arms and legs are made of jelly. But the Lord supports you just as he supported the Israelites in the wilderness. You read how the Lord instructed Moses to say to the Israelites, "You yourselves have seen what I did to Egypt, and how I carried you on eagles' wings and brought you to myself" (Exodus 19:4). The Lord rescued his people from Pharaoh and the armies of Egypt and brought them safely through the wilderness to Mount Sinai and eventually to the Promised Land. Like an eagle carries its young on its wings, so the Lord carried and sustained his people, who would have been in desperate straits without him. How comforting and reassuring it is for you to ride along on the Lord's strong wings!

As they were about to enter the Promised Land, Moses pronounced a blessing on the 12 tribes. He said, "The eternal God is your refuge, and underneath are the everlasting arms" (Deuteronomy 33:27). Where will you turn for protection and safety and security? The police? The rescue squad? The fire department? Other government agencies? None can offer absolute protection. How comforting it is to know that "the eternal God is your refuge." As you travel through life, no matter where you go, no matter what you do, the arms of him who exists from everlasting to everlasting are supporting you.

What wonderful assurances the Lord gave his people Israel! How comforting to know that those promises still apply! Speaking to his people Israel through the prophet Isaiah, the Lord says, "You are my servant; I have chosen you and have not rejected you. So do not fear, for I am with you; do not be dismayed, for I am your God. I will strengthen you and help you; I will uphold you with my righteous right hand" (41:9,10). You realize that in Christ Jesus, God has chosen you to be his own from all eternity, and because you belong to him, you have nothing to fear. He is with you constantly. He who is the maker of heaven and earth is concerned about everything that happens to you, and he promises to give you the strength and the help you need in every situation.

Sometimes you feel as though you can't go on, you can't handle a situation. It is then especially that God assures you he will hold you up, he will sustain and support you. "Even to your old age and gray hairs I am he, I am he who will sustain you. I have made you and I will carry you; I will sustain you and I will rescue you" (Isaiah 46:4)—a wonderful promise that includes you too! You've noticed a few gray hairs lately. You realize you're getting older. But just as the Lord has sustained you to this point in your life, so he will guard and keep you for the remainder of your time on earth. You are not the result of a biological accident or an evolutionary process. God made you. And since he made you, he will also carry you along through life. He will uphold and sustain you every moment. In times of trouble he will rescue you.

Yes, God cares for you. It's the assurance you have because of his love for you in Christ Jesus. It's the special promise he makes to those he has declared to be just and righteous because of Christ's innocent life and death. That's why you realize you can join David in saying, "I was young and now I am old, yet I have never seen the righteous forsaken or their children begging bread. For the LORD loves the just and will not forsake his faithful ones" (Psalm 37:25,28). God provides for you. He protects you. He sustains you. That's what God's providence is all about.

# 2

# The Aspects of God's Providence

The sun is shining brightly overhead. A few clouds float gently in the brilliant blue sky. You can hear the birds chirping. You can smell the evergreens. Up ahead you see a stately white mansion. Ornate pillars grace the front entrance. The building seems to stretch far into the distance. Over the entrance in shiny gold letters is the word "Life." You open the door and go inside. Everything is white and bright. The walls, the ceiling, and even the thick, plush carpet under your feet are white.

In front of you are a number of hallways and corridors. Off to your right are four doors. The sign over them says "Entertainment." As you look more closely, you see that door number 1 is labeled "TV"; door 2, "Books"; door 3,

"Movies"; and door 4, "Theme Parks." You think about which door to open. You have rarely found anything good to watch on TV. Occasionally you enjoy a movie. You're too old for theme parks. You decide to enter the door labeled "Books."

Ahead, you see four more doors, over which is the word "Travel." Door number 1 is labeled "Europe"; door 2, "Asia"; door 3, "South America"; and door 4, "Outer Space." Again you need to choose. "Outer Space" is out. That would be more excitement than your heart could handle. You decide on Europe. So many fascinating countries. So much history there.

Suddenly you find yourself in a small room from which there is only one exit. The exit is labeled "Doing God's Will." As you go through this door, you find yourself in a room in which are all kinds of people who need your help. Some are sick, some poor, some hungry, some troubled. Others are friendless. You have to get down on your knees to help some; you get dirty as you help others. Not everyone appreciates what you're doing. Some even call you names.

As you walk further into this room, all sorts of temptations dart in front of you and slink around you. There's covetousness, greed, envy, jealousy, lust. It's not easy; you have to fight your way through them all.

Again ahead of you there's only one door. It says "Worship." As you go through this door, you meet some people who invite you to pray. Others invite you to sing songs of praise. Others ask you to receive the Lord's Supper. Others encourage you to hear and study the Bible.

Once again there's only one door out of this room, and it's labeled "Witness." In this room people ask you what you believe. Some are your friends and relatives. Others are people you don't even know. You want to tell all of them that Jesus died for their sins.

The next door is labeled "Persecution, Suffering, and Trouble." You don't want to go this way, but you don't have a choice. You can't turn back, and there's no other way to go. In this room people are saying, "You're a fool for believing the things you do." "Do you think you're better than everyone else? Is that why you won't join the crowd and have some fun?" They say all sorts of other things. Some things are nasty, some hurtful, some offensive. And then you get sick. You experience pain. You suffer financial setbacks. You have other problems. But it's not a long room. You soon find the exit.

As you leave this room, you realize you're coming to the end of your tour. Ahead of you are two corridors. One is very wide. The carpet is worn. It's obvious that many have traveled this way. The other corridor is extremely narrow, but it's the way you want to go because in the distance you can see a door labeled "Heaven."

Before you go down this corridor, you turn around to see where you've been. It has been a long journey through this mansion called Life. It has taken a long time.

Wait a minute! Do you see that? You left tracks on the plush, white carpet. At first you're concerned that your shoes were dirty, but then you realize that those are just indentations left by your feet. And then you notice something else. You see a second set of footprints alongside every one of your footprints. Even though you couldn't see him, you know that those are the footprints of your Savior Jesus. He was with you all the way through life. But as you look back, you see that there was only one set of tracks when you went through the room labeled "Persecution, Suffering, and Trouble." You wonder why Jesus left you all alone when you needed him most. Why wouldn't he be with you especially in times of persecution, suffering, and trouble? And then it becomes clear that he didn't leave you. There's only one set of tracks because he was carrying you. That's why you were able to make it. That's why you had feelings of peace and contentment even when things were at their worst. Jesus carried you!

Suddenly you wake up. It was so vivid, so real—but only a dream. You begin to wonder what caused it. Was it the plaque at your aunt and uncle's home with the poem entitled "Footprints in the Sand"? Then you recall the sermon you heard at your nephew's confirmation last spring about how living for Christ is like a journey. There was that antebellum mansion you toured on your vacation last summer. Probably the rich snack before bedtime had something to do with it too!

The dream leads you to think about how life is a journey. As you travel through life, the Lord is with you every step of the way, providing for you and preserving your life, concurring with what you do, and directing your steps.

### Preservation

No matter which door you entered in your dream, you managed to keep on going. It reminds you that God is preserving your life. Just as strawberries or other fruits and vegetables are preserved, so God preserves you. He keeps you from spoiling.

A number of words in Scripture give insights into this concept of preservation. One Hebrew word means to guard, protect, and maintain. It's sometimes used in reference to a monument. Monuments on a Civil War battlefield, for example, help preserve the memory of what happened there. The word is used in Psalm 12 where the Lord says, "I will now arise. . . . I will *protect* them from those who malign them" (verse 5). And then David responds, "O LORD, you will keep us safe and *protect* us from such people forever" (verse 7). In Psalm 31 David says, "In you, O LORD, I have taken refuge" (verse 1). One of the reasons he gives for doing so is "the LORD *preserves* the faithful" (verse 23). Because the Lord does that you can "be strong and take heart" (verse 24).

In Psalm 32, one of the psalms of repentance, David speaks about the assurance of the forgiveness for the guilt of his sin, and then he says to the Lord, "You are my hiding place; you will *protect* me from trouble and surround me with songs of deliverance" (verse 7). In Psalm 140 David prays, "Rescue me, O LORD, from evil men; *protect* me from men of violence. Keep me, O LORD, from the hands of the wicked; *protect* me from men of violence" (verses 1,4).

Another Hebrew word that gives insights into the meaning of preservation can be translated "to keep alive" or "let live." In giving the law of the Lord to the people of Israel, Moses said, "The LORD commanded us to obey all these decrees and to fear the LORD our God, so that we might always prosper and be *kept alive*, as is the case today" (Deuteronomy 6:24). The Lord had preserved his people through all their wanderings in the desert. He had kept them alive.

When the Israelites returned from the Babylonian captivity and rebuilt the city of Jerusalem and the temple, they prayed in part, "You alone are the LORD. You made the heavens, even the highest heavens, and all their starry host, the earth and all that is on it, the seas and all that is in them. You give life to everything, and the multitudes of heaven worship you" (Nehemiah 9:6). The One who created all things is also the One who gives life to everything, who preserves all life.

Another Hebrew word means to guard in the sense of "building a hedge about." It's the word David uses when he prays, "*Keep me safe*, O God, for in you I take refuge" (Psalm 16:1). Concerning the one who "has regard for the weak," David says, "The LORD delivers him in times of trouble. The LORD will *protect* him and preserve his life" (Psalm 41:1,2). The Lord "*guards* the lives of his faithful ones" (Psalm 97:10). "The LORD *protects* the simple-hearted" (Psalm 116:6). "The LORD *watches over* all who love him" (Psalm 145:20). "The LORD *watches over* the alien and sustains the fatherless and the widow" (Psalm 146:9). "He guards the course of the just and *protects* the way of his faithful ones" (Proverbs 2:8).

In challenging the people of Israel to serve the Lord rather than the idols of the nations, Joshua said, "It was the LORD our God himself who brought us and our fathers up out of Egypt, from that land of slavery, and performed those great signs before our eyes. He protected us on our entire journey and among all the nations through which we traveled" (Joshua 24:17). Time and again the Lord guarded his people from their enemies and from natural disasters in the wilderness. He built a hedge about them.

Another Hebrew word means to preserve in the sense of "defending" or "delivering." It literally means to bring safety and salvation, to be a savior. It is the word from which the name Joshua is derived, a name that means savior, as does the name Jesus. In words of praise to the Lord, David says, "Your righteousness is like the mighty mountains, your justice like the great deep. O LORD, you *preserve* both man and beast" (Psalm 36:6). Literally, the Lord preserves people and animals in the sense of saving them, keeping them from danger and preserving their lives. The same word is used to describe the successes the Lord gave King David in his battles against various people. "The LORD *gave* David *victory* wherever he went" (2 Samuel 8:6).

A Greek word in the New Testament has a meaning similar to this Hebrew word. When the angel of the Lord appeared to Joseph in a dream, he said to him concerning Mary, "She will give birth to a son, and you are to give him the name Jesus, because he will *save* his people from their sins" (Matthew 1:21). When Zacchaeus, the man who had climbed the sycamore-fig tree, confessed his faith in Jesus, Jesus said to him in part, "The Son of Man came to seek and to *save* what was lost" (Luke 19:10). Writing to his young friend and coworker Timothy, Paul says, "Here is a trustworthy saying that deserves full acceptance: Christ Jesus came into the world to *save* sinners" (1 Timothy 1:15). From prison Paul writes to Timothy about bad things that have happened to him and about his uncertain future, but then he says, "The Lord will rescue me from every evil attack and will *bring me safely* to his heavenly kingdom" (2 Timothy 4:18). That's the kind of protection the Lord provides for you every day of your life.

Another Greek word in the New Testament literally means to guard, to watch, or to keep an eye on. It's what Jesus prayed for his disciples when he said, "Holy Father, *protect* them by the power of your name. . . . My prayer is not that you take them out of the world but that you *protect* them from the evil one" (John 17:11,15). It's what Paul prayed for the people of Thessalonica when he said, "May your whole spirit, soul and body *be kept* blameless at the coming of our Lord Jesus Christ" (1 Thessalonians 5:23). Jude wrote to "those who have been called, who are loved by God the Father and *kept* by Jesus Christ" (Jude 1).

## Concurrence

In your dream you were walking, and you were opening doors, but the Lord was making that possible for you. That is another aspect of divine providence: concurrence. When two actions are concurrent, they operate at the same time. They run parallel to each other. They act in conjunction with each other. If two people concur about something, they literally "run together" or act together towards a common end or a single effect.

On his second missionary journey Paul was forced to leave the town of Berea because Jews from Thessalonica were agitating the crowds against him. Paul went to Athens, a city famous for hundreds of years for its culture, art, architecture, literature, and philosophy. As Paul walked the streets of Athens, he was greatly disturbed to see that the city was full of idols.

Always determined to proclaim the gospel, Paul went where the people were to be found—the synagogue and the marketplace. In Athens Paul met some Epicurean philosophers, who followed the teachings of Epicurus (341–270 B.C.), who said the gods do not care about mankind and there is no afterlife. The only thing to do, Epicurus said, is try to make the best of life, do what is right and wise, live a life of moderation, and enjoy intellectual pursuits. Epicureanism had been corrupted to become what we today call hedonism: Eat, drink, and be merry for tomorrow we die. Paul also spoke with some Stoic philosophers, who, following the teachings of Zeno (340–265 B.C.), believed the way to find happiness in life was to do one's duty; act reasonably; and when troubles come, keep a stiff upper lip, grin, and bear it.

These philosophers wondered what Paul was trying to say. They suspected he was talking about foreign gods because he was preaching about Jesus and the resurrection. They took Paul to the court of Mars Hill, the Areopagus, and asked him to explain his teachings. Paul could not invite them to open their Bibles so he could show them how Jesus had fulfilled the Old Testament prophecies. That was his method among the Jews and proselytes in the Jewish synagogues. But these people were pagans who worshiped idols; they had no Bibles. Therefore Paul began with the natural knowledge of God, which is available to all people. As he had walked through the streets of Athens, he had found an altar with the inscription "to an unknown god." Paul wished to speak to them about this "god" whom they did not know.

"The God who made the world and everything in it is the Lord of heaven and earth and does not live in temples built by hands" (Acts 17:24). The people should have known about God. The heavens declared his glory. Their consciences testified to his existence. The complexity of the world around them testified to God as the one who had made everything.

Paul continued, "[God] is not served by human hands, as if he needed anything, because he himself gives all men life and breath and everything else" (verse 25). God does not need humans so he can exist or function. He is the one who created people, gives man life, and makes it possible for them to continue to exist. That is true not only of people but of everything else as well, all animals, plants, and the entire universe.

"From one man he made every nation of men, that they should inhabit the whole earth; and he determined the times set for them and the exact places where they should live" (verse 26). God made the first human beings, and all the people in the world are descended from that first couple. God brings people into the world at a certain time and place. God determines the length of their lives. All this is evident from nature. From their natural knowledge of God these men of Athens could understand everything Paul was saying.

God's purpose in planting this knowledge of himself in the hearts of people was so that they might come to know him. "God did this so that men would seek him and perhaps reach out for him and find him, though he is not far from each one of us" (verse 27). They could know that God had created them, that God was concerned about them, that God was present in their world and in their daily lives, and that they could not survive for a single instant unless God concurred with everything they did.

To underscore that this too was something they could know by nature, Paul quoted a Greek poet (probably Epimenedes, who lived about 600 B.C.): "For in him we live and move and have our being" (verse 28). Without God they could not live for a moment. They could not breathe. Their hearts could not beat and pump blood through their veins. They could not lift a hand or move a foot. They could not see or hear or speak. Without God they could not even exist.

Paul was not saying that all is God and God is all. He was not teaching pantheism. God is completely separate from everything he has made. Yet nothing can happen without his concurrence. God is involved in every activity and every action. The result is produced not by God alone nor by creature alone; the result is produced not in part by God and in part by creature; rather, every activity, everything that occurs is a joint action of both God and creature. This is a great mystery that brings many questions to mind. If God concurs in everything I do, can I really be held responsible for the bad things I do? Is it proper to say that God concurs in everything, even in evil actions? How does the human will play into the picture? These matters need further exploration.

### Direction

In your dream you could sense that your journey through that mansion was being guided and directed. That is still another aspect of divine providence: direction. God directs and governs everything that happens. He directs the entire universe. Galaxies, stars, planets, black holes, and whatever else might be in outer space are under God's direction. He governs everything on earth from mighty nations and rulers to one-celled creatures too small to be seen except under a microscope. That's a comforting thought. Nothing operates on its own. God is in control. Events in our lives are not determined by luck or chance. God is in control of everything that happens.

The prophet Jeremiah once prayed, "I know, O LORD, that a man's life is not his own; it is not for man to direct his steps" (Jeremiah 10:23). We are not independent creatures. We are totally dependent on God for everything. We cannot even put one foot in front of the other without God. God must direct and govern our every step. The Hebrew word used here in Jeremiah means to ordain, to order, to establish, to set fast. Literally, it means to stand perpendicular, to be erect.

You think of when your children were learning to walk. At first they couldn't stand erect unless you supported them. They couldn't keep their balance unless you held onto their fingers. They couldn't walk unless you walked along with them and helped them. That's similar to how God directs our steps. The writer of Proverbs uses the same word when he says, "In his heart a man plans his course, but the LORD *determines* his steps" (16:9).

Another Hebrew word depicting God's governance and direction of all things means "to make straight or even." Addressing his son, the writer of Proverbs says, "In all your ways acknowledge him, and he will *make* your paths *straight* [or will direct your paths]" (3:6). Through his prophet Isaiah the Lord speaks about the king he will raise up to deliver his people from Babylonian captivity: "I will raise up Cyrus in my righteousness: I will *make* all his ways *straight*" (45:13). God would so govern and direct things that King Cyrus would release the Jews from captivity. God governs and directs everything that happens. The word is even used in reference to the forces of nature. Elihu says to Job, "He [the Lord] *unleashes* his lightning beneath the whole heaven and sends it to the ends of the earth" (Job 37:3).

There are many references to how God directed and governed his people Israel in the wilderness. At the end of a psalm praising God for his guidance and deliverance, Asaph says, "You led your people like a flock" (77:20). In a song recited in the hearing of the entire assembly of Israel, Moses says: "He [the Lord] guarded him [his people, Jacob] as the apple of his eye, like an eagle that stirs up its nest and hovers over its young, that spreads its wings to catch them and carries them on its pinions. The LORD alone led him; no foreign god was with him" (Deuteronomy 32:10-12). As the Lord guided and directed Israel of old, so he guides and directs your life and the lives of all his children today.

You think about the guided tour you once took through a famous mansion. (That time it was not a dream!) The guide directed your every step. She led you from room to room on every floor as she told you about all the things you were seeing. But as thorough a guide as she was, her direction was nothing compared to how the Lord directs every detail of our lives. It's another amazing example of how much he cares for us.

# 3

# The Scope of God's Providence

You get out of bed and look out the window. It rained overnight. The early spring morning is fresh and cool; the sun is shining brightly. After getting dressed, you decide to take a walk. As you step outside you smell the fresh air; you hear the birds chirping; you see the freshly washed grass and trees, with beads of moisture hanging from them. As you take in a long, deep breath, you think about how God is providing for everything you see, hear, and smell and about how God is providing for you.

### In Jesus all things hold together

You think about how Scripture even assures us that Jesus our Savior provides for all things. In the opening chapter of his letter to the Colossians, Paul speaks about the supremacy of Christ. He says that Christ "is the image of the invisible God" (1:15) in whom God has made himself known by entering human flesh and living among men. He is "the firstborn over all creation," Paul says (verse 15), thus asserting Christ's superiority and primacy over all. And then Paul says something truly remarkable. He says that "by him [Jesus] all things were created: things in heaven and on earth" (verse 16) and that "in him [Jesus] all things hold together" (verse 17). Jesus not only created everything you're seeing on this spring morning, but he is even causing everything to "hold together." Jesus is keeping everything, absolutely everything, from falling apart. All that you're seeing, God is causing to grow, move, and remain alive and healthy—plants, animals, people—everything!

### In his hand is the life of every creature

But come now. Is Jesus really providing for those gnats that suddenly swarm around you? Is Jesus really providing for those bright yellow dandelions growing in your yard? Isn't that too trivial for the Lord of heaven and earth? The church father Jerome thought so. He once wrote: "It is an absurd detraction of the majesty of God to say that God knows every moment how many gnats are born and how many die; how many bedbugs, fleas, and flies there are on earth, what number of fishes live in the water. . . . While we make his power concern itself with most insignificant creatures, we are unfair to ourselves by assuming a like providence extending over rational and irrational creatures."[1] Poor Jerome! He should be here with you on this lovely spring morning.

Jerome should have spent a little more time listening to Job. Job said: "Ask the animals, and they will teach you, or the birds of the air, and they will tell you; or speak to the earth, and it will teach you, or let the fish of the sea inform you. Which of all these does not know that the hand of the LORD has done this? In his hand is the life of every creature and the breath of all mankind" (12:7-10).

Jerome should have paid closer attention to the psalms. In Psalm 104 the author says that the creatures of the earth and sea look to the Lord: "These all look to you to give them their food at the proper time. When you give it to them, they gather it up; when you open your hand, they are satisfied with good things. When you hide your face, they are terrified; when you take away their breath, they die and return to the dust" (verses 27-29). In Psalm 145 David says, "The LORD is good to all; he has compassion on all he has made. The eyes of all look to you, and you give them their food at the proper time. You open your hand and satisfy the desires of every living thing" (verses 9,15,16). Two psalms later Jerome could have read that the Lord "covers the sky with clouds; he supplies the earth with rain and makes grass grow on the hills. He provides food for the cattle and for the young ravens when they call" (147:8,9).

We can understand that the Roman author Cicero would write, "The gods care for the great things and neglect the minor things." It's difficult to understand, though, how a theologian like Jerome, who translated the Bible into Latin in about A.D. 400, could say what he did.

As you walk down the street, you notice your neighbor's rock garden. He has even installed a little water fountain that splashes into a pool below. Is the Lord providing for these rocks and that water? Yes, "in him all things hold together" (Colossians 1:17). You wave to your paperboy as he rides by on his bike. His bag is full. He has just started his paper route. Your paper is going to be late this morning. Is the Lord providing for those papers and that canvass bag and the metal, plastic, and rubber of that bike? Yes, "in him all things hold together." The Lord provides not only for animate things but for inanimate things as well: your tennis shoes, your walking shorts, your eyeglasses, the money in your pocket. "In him all things hold together."

### God clothes the grass of the field

You notice that the young maple trees planted along the boulevard to take the place of the stately elms that died are doing well. Mrs. Smith's crocuses and daffodils are blooming. Her tulips can't be far behind. Thanks to the rain the past couple days, the grass is lush and green. You're going to have to mow your lawn again even though you mowed it just three days ago. Is the Lord concerned about the trees, flowers, and grass? Indeed he is! In the Sermon on the Mount Jesus taught that we don't need to worry because if the Lord is concerned about lilies and grass, he will surely also take care of us. Jesus said, "And why do you worry about clothes? See how the lilies of the field grow. They do not labor or spin. Yet I tell you that not even Solomon in all his splendor was dressed like one of these. If that is how God clothes the grass of the field, which is here today and tomorrow is thrown into the fire, will he not much more clothe you, O you of little faith?" (Matthew 6:28-30).

In a sermon on these words of Jesus, Luther said, "The little flowers stand there and put us to shame by becoming our teachers. Thank you, little flowers, you who are eaten by cows and are so highly exalted by God that you become our masters and teachers. For shame that the earth carries us! If this is an honor for us, I do not know what honor is.

We must confess that the most insignificant little flower, which the cattle tread underfoot, is to turn out to be our schoolmaster."[2]

### Look at the birds of the air

The birds love this beautiful spring morning. At least they sound as if they do. You've got to find out about that bird that sits on the telephone wire in your backyard. He has a brown body and a red head, and his song is particularly lovely. You just wish that he started singing a little later than 4:30 A.M.! Speaking of birds, when you stepped out on the patio before your walk, a robin started making a racket. You soon learned why. In the evergreen she had made a nest in which you saw a couple young ones waiting for their breakfast. Breakfast would be worms, of course. Worms! You had never seen so many worms as you had the other morning after the rain. The streets and sidewalks were thick with long, slimy angleworms and nightcrawlers trying to escape from drowning.

As you walk along, you detect motion to your left. A fox terrier is racing toward you, eyeing your ankle but not making a sound. At the last instant he is pulled up short by the rope tied to the stake in the middle of the yard. Only then does he start to bark.

Maybe you need a dog—a dog that barks before it attacks! Maybe that would scare off the rabbits and the deer that have started to nibble away at the seedlings sprouting in your garden.

Does the Lord care about birds and dogs and rabbits and deer—and worms? Indeed he does! Even grackles and ravens. The Lord asked Job, "Who provides food for the raven when its young cry out to God and wander about for lack of food?" (38:41). The obvious answer is that the

Lord himself provides that food. In the Sermon on the Mount Jesus invited his disciples to "look at the birds of the air; they do not sow or reap or store away in barns, and yet your heavenly Father feeds them. Are you not much more valuable than they?" (Matthew 6:26).

In a sermon on these words of Jesus, Luther said: "The birds fly about before our eyes. We may well take off our hats to them and, with little credit to ourselves, say: My dear doctor, I must confess that I do not possess the ability you possess. You sleep in your little nest at night without any worry. In the morning you arise, are joyous and of good cheer, sit on a tree and sing, praise, and thank God. Then you go in search of your food and find it. For shame! Why have I, old fool that I am, not learned to do the same thing—I, who have so much reason to do so? . . . And yet we cannot stop this shameful worrying."[3]

When Jesus sent out the 12 disciples to preach the message of the kingdom, he assured them that they would have nothing to fear—even from those who might want to kill them. He said, "Are not two sparrows sold for a penny? Yet not one of them will fall to the ground apart from the will of your Father. And even the very hairs of your head are all numbered. So don't be afraid; you are worth more than many sparrows" (Matthew 10:29-31). Sparrows. They must be some of the most prolific birds there are. You hadn't even thought of them before, but now you realize there are more sparrows in your neighborhood than all other birds combined. Yet the Lord is concerned about each one of these sparrows. And if he's concerned about them, won't he be even more concerned about you?

Yes, that's the wonderful truth Jesus emphasizes again and again. The Lord is concerned about plants and animals, and since he is, we can be assured that he is even more concerned about us.

### He watches all who live on earth

As you walk along, you realize that two more lots have been sold. Several new homes have recently been constructed in the next block. The neighborhood is growing. It's getting crowded. But, you say to yourself, this is nothing compared to China and India, where over half the world's people live. Does the Lord care for all those billions of people? What about the people in Africa? Many are starving there. Does the Lord not care as much for them? The psalmist makes clear that God cares for all people: "From heaven the LORD looks down and sees all mankind; from his dwelling place he watches all who live on earth—he who forms the hearts of all, who considers everything they do" (33:13-15).

The Lord cares for all people regardless of race, nationality, age, or gender. The apostle Paul made that clear as he spoke to the men of Athens. They didn't know the message of the Scriptures—they didn't even have the Scriptures—but they should have known that God exists. They should have understood that God made the world and everything in it. They should have realized that God provides for his creatures. Their natural knowledge of God told them that, and Paul reaffirmed that natural knowledge of God as a point of contact with them and as a prelude for sharing the gospel of Christ with them. Paul said, "From one man he made every nation of men, that they should inhabit the whole earth; and he determined the times set for them and the exact places where they should live" (Acts 17:26).

The Lord provides for *all* people? Even for that teenager recently arrested for drug possession? Even for that man who just got his third drunk-driving ticket? Even for that woman who has been accused of child abuse? Yes, even for them. Doesn't it sometimes seem that things go better for people like that than for law-abiding citizens? The psalm writer Asaph felt that way. He said: "I envied the arrogant when I saw the prosperity of the wicked. They have no struggles; their bodies are healthy and strong. They are free from the burdens common to man; they are not plagued by human ills" (73:3-5).

Is that fair? Why should God provide for them? Why should God do anything for the wicked? Why doesn't he just leave them on their own? Amazingly God provides for all. Jesus said, "Your Father in heaven . . . causes his sun to rise on the evil and the good, and sends rain on the righteous and the unrighteous" (Matthew 5:45).

Throughout the history of the world God has provided for the believers and the unbelievers. No one could have survived for an instant if God had not been caring for him. God provided for the pharaohs of Egypt and the rulers of ancient Mesopotamia. God cared for Alexander the Great and Julius Caesar. God even gave Hitler and Stalin everything they needed for their bodies and lives. God has provided for all human beings from the beginning of time to the present day, and he promises to take care of all people until the end of the world.

That was what Paul wanted the people of Lystra to understand, although as in Athens he had an ulterior motive in mind. In Lystra was a man crippled from his birth. The man had never walked. People knew that. So when Paul healed the man, the crowd went wild. They shouted that the gods had come down to them in human form. Barnabas they called Zeus (the chief Greek god), and Paul they called Hermes (the messenger of the Greek gods).

The priest of Zeus even brought bulls and wreaths because he and the crowd wanted to offer sacrifices to them.

Barnabas and Paul would have none of it. They tore their clothes and went among the people shouting: "Men, why are you doing this? We too are only men, human like you. We are bringing you good news, telling you to turn from these worthless things to the living God, who made heaven and earth and sea and everything in them. . . . He has not left himself without testimony: He has shown kindness by giving you rain from heaven and crops in their seasons; he provides you with plenty of food and fills your hearts with joy" (Acts 14:15,17). God provides for all people. He always has; he always will. God is the Lord of history. Though we don't see him in operation, though he hides behind a mask, as it were, yet we know that he is present. The rain and the sunshine testify to him. Seeds which germinate, sprout, and grow testify to him. Harvests which produce grain which is ground into flour which is made into bread which nourishes our bodies testify to him.

### God's chief concern is the church

You've come a long way on your walk—farther than you planned. You can see your church just down the block. What a beautiful church! The stone exterior has a pointed steeple housing a magnificent bell. God takes care of churches too. You remember the kitchen fire last year. Somebody had forgotten to unplug one of the coffeepots after Bible class. You know it wasn't just luck that led the custodian to return to church after dinner to check on the lights. He smelled the smoke, discovered the fire, and extinguished it before any major damage was done.

God also takes care of the church in the sense of the assembly of all those who believe in Jesus as their Savior.

This is the invisible church because only God can see faith, which exists in the hearts of people. Only God can see those who are in this church.

Those in this church have the assurance that because God is in control, nothing can ever happen but what serves his good purpose for them. That's what Paul wrote to the Roman Christians: "We know that in all things God works for the good of those who love him, who have been called according to his purpose" (8:28). What a promise! In everything that happens in our lives, even in the things we consider mundane and unimportant, God is at work to bless us. God even governs troubles and problems so that they serve his purpose for us. God does that because he desires to see us safely through this life, keep us in the saving faith, and take us to himself in heaven.

How comforting it is to know that God is controlling everything for our good. But God has gone even farther. He has also assigned angels to watch over us. The psalmist writes that the Lord "will command his angels concerning you to guard you in all your ways" (Psalm 91:11). Imagine! Around us and with us at all times are angels to protect us. You were lost in thought a moment ago and almost stepped in front of that garbage truck. Why didn't you? What held you back? Or perhaps we should ask *who* held you back? The writer to the Hebrews says, "Are not all angels ministering spirits sent to serve those who will inherit salvation?" (1:14). Yes, angels are present to serve us on our way to heaven. They protect us; they keep us from danger; they watch over us in every step we take. God only knows how many times we have been helped and even had our lives spared because of angels.

Aren't there evil angels around us too? Indeed there are, but God is also protecting us from them. Among other things the demons would like us to suffer physical harm. But God and his angels are present to keep this from happening. Jesus once asked his disciples who people were saying he was. They replied that some thought he was John the Baptist; others that he was Elijah; still others that he was Jeremiah or one of the prophets. Then Jesus asked them who they thought he was. Peter answered, "You are the Christ, the Son of the living God" (Matthew 16:16). Referring to this rocklike confession, Jesus then said, "I tell you that you are Peter, and on this rock I will build my church, and the gates of Hades will not overcome it" (verse 18). Jesus' church consists of those who together with Peter confess that Jesus is the Son of the living God. The "gates of Hades," that is, the devil and all his evil angels, cannot and will not overcome this invisible church of believers. God will see to that.

It's time to head home. You've been out far longer than usual. The beautiful spring morning has been made even more beautiful by the assurance that God is present and providing for all he has made. He's providing for the birds chirping merrily as they fly overhead. He's providing for the squirrel that just scurried up the tree. He's providing for the rabbit that just bounded off at your approach. He's providing for the ants busily building up their hill as they clear out tunnels beneath the sidewalk. Even the sidewalk is there because "in him all things hold together" (Colossians 1:17). The grass, dandelions, bushes, trees, flowers—all are living, growing testimonies to the providence of God.

You exchange a cheery "good morning" with your neighbor. He doesn't go to church. As far as you know, he's not a Christian. Yet the Lord also provides for him. The Lord provides for all the people in your community, in your state, and throughout the world whether they are believers or not. The Lord has provided for all people throughout the history of the world. But what a special comfort you have as a believer in Jesus. Not only is God providing for you, he is also making everything that happens serve a good purpose for you, and he's sending his angels to watch over you in everything you do. Those are his special promises for all believers.

One more thought crosses your mind as you arrive home. If God cares for plants, animals, inanimate things, people, and especially believers—so should you.

# 4

# God's Providence and Secondary Causes

A new house is nearing completion down the block. Every day over the past several months you have watched the construction with fascination. First they came in with the backhoe and dug the hole. Then they poured the footings and constructed the foundation. You were amazed to see how quickly and expertly the blocklayers worked. The 2- by 6-foot walls went up in one day. The carpenters measured, sawed, and nailed the boards into place. Once the prefabricated roof trusses had been put into place you could see the shape of the house clearly. Windows and doors were installed. Though you couldn't always see what was happening, you knew that electricians, plumbers, and heating specialists were busy inside getting the house ready for people to move in. You marveled at the unique ability each of the laborers possessed. From start to finish, the house was a piece of expert workmanship.

Who really built that house? Psalm 127 says, "Unless the LORD builds the house, its builders labor in vain" (verse 1). The Lord was building that house. How so? The Lord gave the architect the mind to design that house. The Lord made it possible for someone to invent the back-hoe to dig the hole. The Lord gave the blocklayers arms and hands with which to manipulate the trowels, blocks, and cement. The Lord made it possible for the carpenters to figure out the length of the boards and to wield a hammer and operate a saw. The Lord made the materials for the blocks and cement. The Lord made the trees from which the lumber was taken. If it hadn't been for the Lord, the builders would have been laboring in vain. So it has ever been with the construction of houses.

Psalm 127 continues: "Unless the LORD watches over the city, the watchmen stand guard in vain" (verse 1). How many times haven't you had to tell your children to play more quietly, reminding them that the policeman two doors away was sleeping? Officer Stein is a pleasant man, but he has let it be known that he needs peace and quiet during the daytime because he patrols at night. You have seen him late at night in the patrol car, driving the streets of the city to see that people obey the laws. How grateful you are for police officers like Officer Stein. They make your city a safe place to live.

But who is it really who is guarding the city? The psalm says the Lord "watches over the city." If it weren't for the Lord, police officers would patrol the streets in vain.

It is God who provides. He simply uses construction workers and police officers to serve his purposes. We can speak of them as secondary causes. The Lord is the primary cause of providence.

God is the one who "gives all men life and breath and everything else" (Acts 17:25). People do the living. People do the breathing. But God makes it possible for them to live and breathe. God is the first cause. "In him we live and move and have our being" (verse 28). We are the ones who move, who place one foot in front of the other. We are the people who exist. But unless God were the primary cause, we could not live or move or exist for a moment.

Deists believe that God made the world and everything in it but then withdrew himself to let things happen on their own. People, they say, are totally responsible for their own accomplishments and their own destinies. God is not taking an active interest. God is not present in the daily lives of people, they say.

Pantheists believe that all is God and God is all, and therefore whatever you do and whatever happens is really God at work. There is no God, they say, apart from what exists.

The Bible does not allow for such ideas. God exists apart from everything he has made, but he is not uninterested or uninvolved. He is the primary cause, the first cause, of everything that is, of everything that happens.

When you took two aspirin yesterday afternoon for your headache, and a half hour later your headache went away, it was really God who caused your headache to disappear. The aspirin were merely the means God used to do it.

You remember how, when you were young, you used to envy your friend who never had to get any shots. You had to get that painful shot for diphtheria, polio, and tetanus—with a needle that seemed about six inches long and half an inch wide—but your friend didn't have to get that shot because his parents didn't believe in such things. At the time you envied him, but since then you've come to realize it was better to get those shots because they were the secondary cause, or means, through which God, the primary cause, would keep you from getting dreadful diseases.

It works the same way with food. The ham sandwich and the bowl of chicken noodle soup you had for lunch were the secondary cause of satisfying your hunger. God was the first cause.

It was God who quenched your thirst a few moments ago. The glass of water was merely the means by which he did it.

God is the one who provides. Aspirin, shots, food, and water are the secondary means God uses to do it. The means are subordinate to God. God does not work some magic on food beforehand so that it nourishes you when you eat it. Rather, he cooperates with the means; God works and the means work so that you are nourished, your thirst is quenched, and your headache is removed.

### The laws of nature

But what about the laws of nature? Aren't there some things that just happen naturally without God, without divine intervention?

Near the end of the 17th century, Isaac Newton published his *Mathematical Principles of Natural Philosophy*, in which he used the key concepts and basic laws of mass, motion, and gravity to provide an explanation for both the movements of the planets and the stars as well as the movements of objects on earth. Newton thus established the basic laws of physics. He was able to account for the orbits of planets and moons, the motion of comets, the motion of falling objects on the earth's surface, weight, ocean tides, and the earth's equatorial bulge. People said he made the universe understandable. He demonstrated that the universe ran automatically according to the action of forces between its parts. He demonstrated that the force of gravity between two objects is proportional to the product of the two masses and inversely proportional to the square of the distance between them. Newton formulated the mathematical laws governing the way colors combine to make up white light and showed how a prism can be used to demonstrate this phenomenon.

The world speaks of these things as "laws of nature." Actually they are evidences of God's will in action for the welfare of his creatures. Nature, even when personified as "Mother Nature," is not the proper explanation for how and why things happen. It is God who does everything.

We say that the grass, flowers, and trees grow naturally and that apple trees produce apples and pear trees produce pears naturally, but the Bible says this happens because God said, "Let the land produce vegetation: seed-bearing plants and trees on the land that bear fruit with seed in it, according to their various kinds" (Genesis 1:11).

We say that night naturally follows day, that the sun rises and sets. We speak about the phases of the moon. We talk about one season naturally following another. Spring gives way to summer; summer gives way to fall; fall gives way to winter. The days and years continue to go by as they always have. But the Bible says these things happen because God said, "Let there be lights in the expanse of the sky to separate the day from the night, and let them serve as signs to mark seasons and days and years, and let them be lights in the expanse of the sky to give light on the earth" (verses 14,15).

We say there is going to be good fishing at a certain lake because it is well stocked with walleyes and northerns. We expect to have turkey for Thanksgiving and eggs with our bacon in the morning because there naturally continue to be a great number of turkeys, and chickens provide eggs. But these things happen, the Bible says, because God said, "Be fruitful and increase in number and fill the water in the seas, and let the birds increase on the earth" (verse 22).

We naturally expect to have a time to plant seeds in the spring and to have a harvest in the fall, but these things happen because God said, "As long as the earth endures, seedtime and harvest, cold and heat, summer and winter, day and night will never cease" (8:22).

We speak about natural causes. We say that when we eat, it naturally happens that our hunger is satisfied and we are nourished. The same thing happens when we feed the dog or the cat. The natural cause of the hunger being satisfied is the food that is eaten. But the Bible says this happens because God said, "I give you every seed-bearing plant on the face of the whole earth and every tree that has fruit with seed in it. They will be yours for food. And to all the beasts of the earth and all the birds of the air and all the creatures that move on the ground—everything that has the breath of life in it—I give every green plant for food" (1:29,30).

We say that it naturally rains when the atmospheric conditions are right, but the Bible says it rains because God "waters the mountains from his upper chambers; the earth is satisfied by the fruit of his work. He makes grass grow for the cattle, and plants for man to cultivate—bringing forth food from the earth" (Psalm 104:13,14).

We watch the squirrels gathering nuts and the birds eating seeds in the lawn, and we say that is how nature takes care of the creatures, but the Bible says it is really the Lord who provides sustenance for all: "The eyes of all look to you, and you give them their food at the proper time. You open your hand and satisfy the desires of every living thing" (Psalm 145:15,16).

We speak about natural causes and the laws of nature, but really it is God who has established everything and makes everything happen as it does. "When he established the force of the wind and measured out the waters, when he made a decree for the rain and a path for the thunderstorm, then he looked at wisdom and appraised it; he confirmed it and tested it" (Job 28:25-27).

Natural laws continue to be effective because of God's promise and because of his word and presence. Just as bread nourishes us today, so manna nourished the Israelites in the wilderness. Moses reminded them, "He [the Lord] humbled you, causing you to hunger and then feeding you with manna, which neither you nor your fathers had known, to teach you that man does not live on bread alone but on every word that comes from the mouth of the LORD" (Deuteronomy 8:3). The writer to the Hebrews says, "The Son is the radiance of God's glory and the exact representation of his being, sustaining all things by his powerful word" (1:3).

The Lord makes it possible for us to continue to speak, hear, and see. When Moses was reluctant to go to Egypt to lead God's people from bondage, he used the excuse that he was not eloquent, that he was slow of speech and tongue, but the Lord said to him, "Who gave man his mouth? Who makes him deaf or mute? Who gives him sight or makes him blind? Is it not I, the LORD?" (Exodus 4:11).

Success in battle or business or life in general is not something that happens naturally but, rather, because of

God's word and presence. Saul's son Jonathan, when considering attacking some Philistines, said to his armorbearer, "Perhaps the LORD will act in our behalf. Nothing can hinder the LORD from saving, whether by many or by few" (1 Samuel 14:6).

Scientists speak of the "unchangeable" laws of nature. Consider, for example, the law of gravity or the law of inertia, which says that objects at rest tend to stay that way unless acted on by an outside force. Or consider the law which says that for every action there is an equal and opposite reaction. Or consider the first law of thermodynamics, which says energy is indestructible, that it can neither be created nor destroyed but simply changes form. Or consider the second law of thermodynamics, which says things progress from a state of relative order to one of disorder and an increasing complexity. But these laws are not immutable. They are rather God's will in action for the welfare of his creatures. "Our God is in heaven; he does whatever pleases him" (Psalm 115:3). "The LORD does whatever pleases him, in the heavens and on the earth, in the seas and all their depths" (Psalm 135:6). God governs everything according to his gracious, good will. He who made the laws of nature is above them. He is not bound by them. He can change them as he wishes.

### Angels

The secondary means God uses to provide for people may sometimes be angels. Because Daniel had refused to bow down and pray to King Darius, he was thrown into a den of lions to be executed. But God spared his life, and Daniel explained to the king how God did it: "My God sent his angel, and he shut the mouths of the lions. They have not hurt me, because I was found innocent in his sight" (Daniel 6:22). God sent angels to provide for Jesus when he was tempted by the devil in the wilderness. "[Jesus] was with the wild animals, and angels attended him" (Mark 1:13). God could have provided for Daniel directly. He could have attended to Jesus himself. Instead, he used angels as his agents to provide for them.

Because Peter and John were preaching about Christ and the resurrection, they were arrested and placed into the public jail. "But during the night an angel of the Lord opened the doors of the jail and brought them out" (Acts 5:19). The Lord could have intervened directly, but instead he used angels to deliver the apostles. Sometime later when King Herod had James, John's brother, put to death with the sword and saw how this pleased the Jews, he seized Peter also and placed him in prison. Peter was bound between two soldiers, and sentries stood guard at the entrance, but that was not a problem for the angel of the Lord who suddenly appeared to deliver Peter from prison (12:7-10).

God sends his angels to deliver not only heroes of faith like Daniel and Peter, but also people like you and me. "Are not all angels ministering spirits sent to serve those who will inherit salvation?" (Hebrews 1:14). What a comfort it is to know that angels are watching over us, guarding us, protecting us, providing for us and that God is using the angels as his secondary agents to accomplish his purposes for us.

### Government

God also uses earthly governments to provide for people. Jehoshaphat, king of Judah, showed that he understood this when he appointed judges in each of the fortified cities of Judah and told them, "Consider carefully what you do, because you are not judging for man but for the LORD, who is with you whenever you give a verdict" (2 Chronicles 19:6). God has established government. He has placed into office presidents, governors, mayors, and police officers to serve as his agents, to provide for and protect the citizens of the country, state, or community. The Bible says concerning the person in authority, "He is God's servant to do you good" (Romans 13:4).

You think about the sign on the side of Officer Stein's squad car. It says, "To Protect and Serve." The thought crosses your mind that it could also say, "On Behalf of God."

### The family

The family is another agency God uses to provide for people. "A father to the fatherless, a defender of widows, is God in his holy dwelling. God sets the lonely in families" (Psalm 68:5,6). God could provide for people directly. Instead, he has instituted the family to serve as his agent.

You think about your immediate family and how you and your wife have cared for your children over the years, how you have cared for each other, and you suddenly see things in a different light. It is really God who has been taking care of your family and using you to do it.

### Miracles

God normally uses secondary means to provide for people. He uses what we call the laws of nature. He uses angels, government, and family to provide for and to protect people. But God doesn't have to use these secondary means. When it suits his purposes, he can suspend the laws of nature and work through miracles.

There were three critical periods in the history of his people Israel when God provided a large number of miracles: (1) when Moses and Aaron were to lead the Israelites out of Egypt, (2) when the prophets Elijah and Elisha spoke out against idolatry, and (3) when Christ and the apostles proclaimed the gospel message. In each period God suspended the laws of nature and made it possible for his servants to perform miracles which authenticated them as servants of God. By suspending the laws of nature, by departing from his normal method of using secondary causes, God provided food for people, protected people, brought healing to people, and even raised people from the dead.

Sometimes people ask, Does God still perform miracles today? We know that God certainly can if he wants. You may have heard of events that certainly seem to transcend the laws of nature, such as a person being completely cured of an otherwise incurable disease, with no known medical explanation. But we also know from Scripture that God has made no promises that believers may expect or demand such miracles.

What's more, Scripture also warns us to be cautious with the claims of people to do miracles. Jesus and the apostles warned that Satan and false teachers will perform counterfeit miracles in an attempt to deceive people.

Paul warned the Thessalonians, "The coming of the lawless one will be in accordance with the work of Satan displayed in all kinds of counterfeit miracles, signs and wonders, and in every sort of evil that deceives those who are perishing (2 Thessalonians 2:9,10). Jesus also warned his disciples, "For false Christs and false prophets will appear and perform great signs and miracles to deceive even the elect—if that were possible" (Matthew 24:24).

Especially when any religious teachers claim to do miracles, the question to consider is not "Are the miracles genuine?" but "Is their teaching fully scriptural?" If it is not, Scripture warns us, "Keep away from them" (Romans 16:17).

Whether you have ever actually witnessed or experienced a miracle or not, when you stop to think about it, you realize that the evidence of God's loving concern for you is around you constantly. Though you find yourself taking it for granted all too often, it is God who is actually providing for you as you eat, drink, and take medicine and as you live in your home, in your community, and with your family. God's care for you is truly amazing!

# 5

# Concurrence

If there is a God, why is there so much evil in the world? You've asked yourself that question more than once. Every day you hear about war, or at least the threat of war, in this or that part of the world. If there is a God, why doesn't he put a stop to war? Why doesn't he prevent all the horrible things connected with wars? Why doesn't he prevent the deaths of thousands of soldiers on the battlefield? the horrible wounds? the psychological and emotional trauma? the killing of innocent civilians—women and children? the destruction of cities, homes, businesses, and parks? the displacement of people? the malnutrition and starvation? Why doesn't he prevent the genocide that is sometimes connected with war? Why would God permit instruments

of mass destruction to be invented? intercontinental ballis-
tic missiles and nuclear warheads? biological and chemical
warfare? Why doesn't God just put an end to all war?

Why doesn't God prevent crime, you wonder. Every
day, especially in the larger cities of our country, one reads
and hears about murders. People are murdered because of
drug deals gone awry or as the result of disagreements that
lead to anger and violence. Why does God permit abuse to
take place? Why does he permit wife or husband battering?
Why does he permit physical or sexual child abuse? Why
are there kidnappings, abduct       es, extortion, thiev-
ery, robbery, and white-collar crime? If there is a God, why
doesn't he prevent these things from happening?

Why doesn't God keep me from sinning, you wonder.
He is all-powerful, and if he is in control of everything,
why doesn't he keep me from thinking sinful thoughts,
speaking unkind words, and neglecting to help and serve
others?

If there is a God, why is there evil? How can he permit
it to happen? How can it continue to happen? Why
doesn't he prevent it from happening? These are questions
the Bible answers as it teaches how God concurs in everything that happens, in evil and in good.

### Concurrence in evil

God concurs in, he goes along with, everything that
happens, even everything that is evil. It perhaps doesn't
seem proper to say that. It maybe even seems blasphemous
to suggest it. But say it we can, and say it we must.

### God forbids evil

It is important to realize that God clearly forbids all
evil. In the Ten Commandments he says: "You shall have

no other gods before me. You shall not misuse the name of the LORD your God. . . . You shall not murder. You shall not commit adultery. You shall not steal. You shall not give false testimony against your neighbor. You shall not covet your neighbor's house . . . or anything that belongs to your neighbor" (Exodus 20:3,7,13-17). Again and again in the Scriptures God forbids evil. Through his prophet Isaiah he says, "Wash and make yourselves clean. Take your evil deeds out of my sight! Stop doing wrong" (1:16). "Let the wicked forsake his way and the evil man his thoughts. Let him turn to the LORD, and he will have mercy on him, and to our God, for he will freely pardon" (55:7).

At the pool of Bethesda, Jesus once healed a man who had been an invalid for 38 years. Later when Jesus found the man at the temple, he said to him, "See, you are well again. Stop sinning or something worse may happen to you" (John 5:14). On another occasion the teachers of the law and the Pharisees brought to Jesus a woman who had been caught in adultery. They wanted to trap Jesus, but Jesus saw through their plans and gave them an answer that caused them to walk away speechless. Then after assuring the woman of forgiveness for her sins, Jesus said to her, "Go now and leave your life of sin" (8:11).

In his epistles the apostle Paul repeatedly warns his readers to turn away from evil. "Therefore do not let sin reign in your mortal body so that you obey its evil desires" (Romans 6:12). "Come back to your senses as you ought, and stop sinning; for there are some who are ignorant of God—I say this to your shame" (1 Corinthians 15:34). "You were taught, with regard to your former way of life, to put off your old self, which is being corrupted by its deceitful desires" (Ephesians 4:22).

The writer to the Hebrews says, "Therefore, since we are surrounded by such a great cloud of witnesses, let us throw off everything that hinders and the sin that so easily entangles, and let us run with perseverance the race marked out for us" (12:1). The apostle Peter writes, "Dear friends, I urge you, as aliens and strangers in the world, to abstain from sinful desires, which war against your soul" (1 Peter 2:11).

Yes, God clearly forbids evil. God does not will evil. He does not desire it. In fact, he frequently prevents it.

### God prevents evil

As Abraham and his family moved from place to place, they once came to live in the area of the Philistines. For a while they stayed in the Philistine city of Gerar and, possibly fearing that the king of Gerar would kill him in order to be able to take his wife Sarah, Abraham said concerning his wife, "She is my sister" (Genesis 20:2). (It was a kind of half-truth because Sarah was Abraham's half sister.) Hearing that, Abimelech, king of Gerar, sent for Sarah and took her into his palace. But God came to Abimelech in a dream one night and told him that he was as good as dead because the woman he had taken was a married woman. Abimelech pleaded his innocence before the Lord, and then God said to him in the dream, "Yes, I know you did this with a clear conscience, and so I have kept you from sinning against me. That is why I did not let you touch her" (verse 6). God does sometimes keep people from sinning. He does sometimes prevent evil from happening.

To prevent evil from happening, God repeatedly told his people Israel to purge evildoers from their midst. Concerning a prophet who wanted the people to follow other gods, God said he must be put to death: "You must purge the evil from among you" (Deuteronomy 13:5). Any of God's people who worshiped other gods were also to be put to death. A person who committed a murder, a rebellious son, a person guilty of fornication, a person guilty of kidnapping—all were to be put to death. In each case the Lord said, "Purge the evil from among you." The stiff penalty for these crimes was intended to prevent people from committing them.

### God uses evil for good

God does not will evil. He does not desire it. But when evil happens, in every case God governs it according to his will. The classic example of that is the story of Joseph. You recall how in their envy and jealousy, the brothers of Joseph had intended to kill him, but then put him into a pit and later sold him into slavery, giving their father, Jacob, the impression that Joseph had been killed by a wild beast. It was evil heaped on evil. The brothers had intended nothing but evil against Joseph, and Joseph continued to experience evil in Egypt, being falsely accused by Potiphar's wife and being thrown into prison. But God used all these evil things to accomplish his good purpose for Joseph and for his people. Later, when Joseph was raised to the position of prime minister, he wisely managed the grain supply so that many people had plenty to eat and even the family of Jacob could come to Egypt for food and eventually settle in the land of Goshen. Joseph recognized how marvelously God's providence had worked when he later said to his brothers, "You intended to harm me, but God intended it for good to accomplish what is now being done, the saving of many lives" (Genesis 50:20).

Also describing how God uses evil for good, the apostle Paul wrote to the Romans, "We know that in all things

God works for the good of those who love him, who have been called according to his purpose" (8:28). "In all things"—in sickness or in health, in want or in plenty, in bad times or in good times—God is at work in our lives to bring about his good purposes for us. We may not always understand what that purpose is (Joseph probably didn't always have a clear understanding of what good could possibly come out of what he was suffering), but we can be assured that God is in control so that his good purposes will always be accomplished. That's how wise and powerful God is.

God forbids evil. He frequently prevents evil from happening. But whenever he permits evil, he always causes it to serve his purposes for us.

### God is not the author of evil

What, then, is meant by saying that God concurs in evil? The word *concur* literally means to act together to a common end or a single effect. It can also mean to approve or to express agreement. It is the first definition we use when referring to God's actions regarding evil. We surely cannot charge God with evil. Moses says concerning God: "He is the Rock, his works are perfect, and all his ways are just. A faithful God who does no wrong, upright and just is he" (Deuteronomy 32:4).

After being delivered from King Saul, David composed a psalm in which he said, "As for God, his way is perfect; the word of the LORD is flawless" (18:30). Another psalm says, "The LORD is upright; he is my Rock, and there is no wickedness in him" (92:15). Other psalms say, "Righteous are you, O LORD, and your laws are right" (119:137); "The LORD is righteous in all his ways and loving toward all he has made" (145:17).

In his Sermon on the Mount, after describing what the life of a believer is to be like, Jesus said, "Be perfect, therefore, as your heavenly Father is perfect" (Matthew 5:48). God is perfect; there is no evil in him, and when we say that he concurs in evil, we are in no way ascribing evil to God.

To say that God concurs in evil does not mean that he is the author of evil. The author of a novel needs to develop a plot, a point of view, characters, dialogue, etc. The author is the one who determines how the story will unfold. He controls his characters. He gives them words to speak and things to do. He determines that a certain character will be the protagonist. Perhaps he will be a villain. In a certain sense we can say that the novelist is the author of the evil about which he writes. But we cannot speak of God as the author of evil. Now certainly we might ask, If God created everything—the universe, angels, and people—and there are evil angels and evil people, then isn't God, at least in a certain sense, the author of evil? To that question we must answer unequivocally, No! Regarding the origin of evil, we can say it was Adam and Eve and before them the devil, but it wasn't God.

When we say that God concurs in evil, we don't mean that he is a kind of accomplice in evil. An accomplice in crime does not necessarily perform the crime himself. He maybe doesn't hold up the bank; he just drives the get-away car. He doesn't sell drugs himself; he sends out those who do. King David probably thought he would not be held responsible for murder if he didn't carry the act out himself. So he arranged for Uriah, with whose wife, Bathsheba, David had had an affair, to be placed in the front line of battle, where he would surely be killed. David didn't actually murder Uriah, but by planning and plotting Uriah's death, he was an accomplice to the murder and was equally guilty (2 Samuel 11:14,15). When we say that God concurs in evil, we do not mean that he is an accomplice in evil, for then surely he would be guilty of evil himself.

### God concurs with the acts, not the evil

How God can concur with evil without being the author or an accomplice in the evil remains a mystery to us. We must conclude that God goes along with evil acts only to the extent that they are acts, but not that they are evil. In our minds we must try to make a difference between the act itself and the evil part of that act. God goes along with the effect of all actions but never the defect connected with those actions. Those who do evil, those who commit crimes can only do so because in God they live and move and have their being (Acts 17:28). God concurs with people's actions not only when they do good, but also when they do evil.

Imagine that a man is planning to hold up a bank. He drives up in front of the bank and gets out of the car with a large briefcase in his hand. As he enters the bank, he puts on a ski mask, goes up to one of the tellers, puts the briefcase on the counter, and says to her, "I want you to fill this briefcase with 20-dollar bills." In order to drive home his point and to force her to do what he wants, he says he has a gun in his pocket. After the briefcase is filled, he picks it up, walks out of the bank, takes off his ski mask, gets in the car, and drives away.

That bank robber couldn't have done any of that unless God was concurring in what he did. He couldn't have driven the car. He couldn't have carried the briefcase. He couldn't have put on the ski mask. He couldn't have spoken to the teller. He couldn't have pretended to have a gun in his pocket. He couldn't have walked out of the bank. He couldn't have gotten into his car and driven away—unless God was concurring in everything he did. But we must conclude that God went along with those actions only to the extent that they were actions, not that they were evil. That man alone was responsible for the evil. In no way could God be held accountable.

### Permission

Sometimes God's concurrence in evil is spoken of as permission. That doesn't mean, however, that God permits evil in the sense that he doesn't care or has no power over evil.

At the time of the Reformation, Martin Luther spoke against indulgences. People could buy pieces of paper that offered them forgiveness for part or all of the temporal, and especially the purgatorial, punishment of their sins. But God's permission of evil is not like an indulgence. It's not as if God says, "Well, people are going to sin anyway, so I might as well indulge them."

God's permission of evil is not a license to sin. People may buy a marriage license, which permits them to get married. People may buy a fishing or hunting license, which permits them to fish or hunt. God's permission of evil does not mean that he is issuing licenses to sin.

Permission is not a weakness in God, as if he can't do anything about evil and so must allow it. It surely is not a defect in God, as if there is one thing he cannot do, and that is prevent evil. Nor is permission the same as indifference, as if God doesn't really care about evil. God hates evil and threatens to punish all who do evil.

What, then, does God's permission of evil mean? You recall how Delilah sought to discover the secret of Samson's great strength. "If anyone ties me with seven fresh thongs . . . I'll become as weak as any other man," Samson said (Judges 16:7). But when the Philistines came, he snapped the thongs as if they were a piece of string. "If anyone ties me securely with new ropes that have never been used, I'll become as weak as any other man," Samson said (verse 11). But again he snapped the ropes off his arms as if they were threads. Again Samson said, "If you weave the seven braids of my head into the fabric on the loom . . . I'll become as weak as any other man" (verse 13). But when the Philistines came, Samson pulled up the pin and the loom along with the fabric. Finally, Samson told Delilah that if his head were shaved, his strength would leave him and he would become as weak as any other man. Samson thought he would be able to shake himself free as before, but this time the Philistines seized Samson, gouged out his eyes, and took him down to Gaza. The Bible says that Samson "did not know that the LORD had left him" (verse 20). Since Samson had turned against the Lord, the Lord permitted him to suffer the consequences of his evil.

When King Saul turned against the Lord, the Spirit of the Lord departed from Saul, and God even permitted an evil spirit to torment Saul (1 Samuel 16:14).

When the people of Israel were unfaithful to the Lord, "he made them an object of horror" (2 Chronicles 30:7). He permitted them to suffer the evil consequences of their wickedness as they were taken captive by the Assyrians. Throughout their history God had wanted to shower his blessings on his people, but so often they would not listen to him, they would not submit to him, and so the Lord said, "I gave them over to their stubborn hearts to follow their own devices" (Psalm 81:12). It happens whenever people reject the Lord. "They will eat the fruit of their ways and be filled with the fruit of their schemes" (Proverbs 1:31).

Because the people of Jerusalem had rejected the prophets and had even refused to accept God's own Son, Jesus said, "Look, your house is left to you desolate" (Matthew 23:38). As the apostle Paul spoke to the people of Lystra about God, who had made the heaven and earth and everything in them, he explained that "in the past, he [God] let all nations go their own way" (Acts 14:16). God didn't want that, he didn't approve of it, but when people rejected him and chose to go contrary to his way, the Lord permitted them to do so. In his epistle to the Romans, Paul speaks about how all people know there is a God from the wonderful things he has made and from their own consciences. But in spite of their natural knowledge of God, people often turn away from God to worship images made with their own hands, and they give themselves over to shameful lusts. Paul says, "Therefore God gave them over in the sinful desires of their hearts to sexual impurity for the degrading of their bodies with one another" (1:24). Since they chose to live a life contrary to God's will, God permitted them to suffer the consequences of their sin; "he gave them over to a depraved mind, to do what ought not to be done" (verse 28).

God does not will what he permits, but he permits it nevertheless. We might speak of it as a kind of negative act. God allows sinners to rush headlong into the sins they have chosen to commit. Judas Iscariot had made plans to betray Jesus into the hands of his enemies. Jesus was aware of that, even as Judas sat there with the other disciples in the upper room on the night Jesus was betrayed. "I tell you the truth, one of you will betray me. . . . The one who has dipped his hand into the bowl with me will betray me" (Matthew 26:21,23). Jesus knew Judas would betray him, but he did not prevent him from doing so. He could have. He could have frozen him to the spot so he couldn't move. He could have caused his legs to wither so he couldn't walk. Instead, he permitted Judas to rush headlong into his sin of betrayal.

When we speak of God concurring in evil, it surely does not mean he causes or encourages evil. The Lord hates evil. David says, "You are not a God who takes pleasure in evil; with you the wicked cannot dwell. The arrogant cannot stand in your presence; you hate all who do wrong. You destroy those who tell lies; bloodthirsty and deceitful men the LORD abhors" (Psalm 5:4-6). When we speak of God concurring in evil, we mean that the evil can only happen as God goes along with the act. God is, however, never responsible for the evil. He always causes that evil to serve his purposes—for believers God uses evil to draw them closer to him, and for unbelievers, to serve as a judgment on them.

### Concurrence in good

God concurs in everything that happens, also in those things we speak of as good. Though we live in a world of sin and wickedness, we regularly see things we would consider good, even among those who are not believers in Jesus. People provide food and clothing for the poor and unfortunate. There are programs to help those who are without work or those who have emotional, psychological, or physical problems. Society has many benefactors who provide beautiful parks, libraries, concert halls, and museums. There are people who gladly lend a helping hand, who give another person the right of way, who open the door for another. These are all things we call good, even though the people who do them may not be Christians. God is concurring in all these things too. None of this would happen unless God were cooperating with it.

Although people cannot earn their way to heaven by anything they do, people do receive earthly, temporal blessings because of the good things they do. The Egyptian pharaoh had commanded the midwives to put to death any Hebrew boy babies they delivered. They refused to do so, and God blessed them for their good deeds. "Because the midwives feared God, he gave them families of their own" (Exodus 1:21). Also today people are blessed for their good deeds. They may be well thought of, they may have a good reputation, or they may enjoy financial success.

There is an added dimension when we speak about the good works of believers. Here God not only concurs in the good deed itself, but the Holy Spirit works the very desire and ability to do it. Speaking about the Philippians' faith and lives as Christians, the apostle Paul says, "For it has been granted to you on behalf of Christ not only to believe on him, but also to suffer for him" (Philippians 1:29), and then he says, "For it is God who works in you to will and to act according to his good purpose" (2:13). God works faith, the ability to suffer, and the desire and ability to do good works. Believers do the good works but must join Paul who also said, "Not that we are competent in ourselves to claim anything for ourselves, but our competence comes from God" (2 Corinthians 3:5). So God not only concurs in the good things believers do, but he also prompts the desire, the ability, and the good deeds themselves.

# 6

# Necessity and Contingency

"Shall I wear the brown or the blue dress?" "Yes," you had said. You answered that way because you hadn't heard the second part of the question. It wasn't the appropriate answer, of course.

"Are you going to get married, or do you intend to remain single?" "Yes" is not the answer a parent expects to hear. It's either one or the other. Either a person will get married or stay single. It's impossible to do both at the same time.

"Shall we go to a fast food restaurant for lunch or to a sit-down restaurant?" Again "yes" is not the answer you want to hear because you can't be two places at once. You must go to one restaurant or the other.

Either/or questions demand a choice. Either one thing or the other is true. Either one or the other thing is to be done. Answering "yes" to an either/or question is usually only possible if a person didn't hear the question, didn't understand the question, didn't want to commit to a decision, or was just trying to be funny.

Except when it comes to a certain question. That question is, Does everything have to happen the way it does, or could things happen otherwise? The only proper answer to that question is, "Yes." Yes, everything does have to happen the way it does. Yes, things could happen otherwise. It depends on the viewpoint. From the viewpoint of necessity, everything has to happen the way it does. From the viewpoint of contingency, things could happen otherwise.

### Christ's death—a necessity

Consider, for example, the most important event in the history of the world: Christ's death on the cross of Calvary. Was it God's will that Christ die on the cross? Or were wicked men responsible for his death? The Bible answers both those questions with a yes.

Jesus had gone with his disciples to Gethsemane. He had invited them to watch and pray with him, but while Jesus prayed, they slept. Judas, the betrayer, came with a large crowd to have Jesus arrested. When the men seized Jesus and arrested him, Peter reached for his sword and struck off the ear of the high priest's servant. Jesus said to Peter, "Put your sword back in its place. . . . Do you think I cannot call on my Father, and he will at once put at my disposal more than twelve legions of angels? But how then would the Scriptures be fulfilled that say it must happen in this way?" (Matthew 26:52-54). Jesus had to be betrayed.

He had to be arrested. He had to suffer. He had to be nailed to a cross. He had to die. The Old Testament Scriptures had said these things would happen. God had determined it. Christ's death was a necessity. It was God's plan from all eternity to save sinners.

After Peter and John healed a beggar at the temple gate called Beautiful, the people came running to see them. Peter called on them to repent and believe in Jesus as their Savior from sin. This, in turn, upset the priests, the captain of the temple guard, and the Saduccees. They were disturbed because Peter and John were teaching that Jesus had risen from the dead. So they seized Peter and John and put them in jail. At the trial before the Sanhedrin Peter said, "Salvation is found in no one else, for there is no other name under heaven given to men by which we must be saved" (Acts 4:12). When commanded not to teach or speak at all about Jesus, Peter and John replied, "We cannot help speaking about what we have seen and heard" (verse 20).

After their release, Peter and John went back to their fellow believers who, on hearing what had happened, raised their voices together in prayer. They said in part, "Indeed Herod and Pontius Pilate met together with the Gentiles and the people of Israel in this city to conspire against your holy servant Jesus, whom you anointed. They did what your power and will had decided beforehand should happen" (verses 27,28). Why did Herod and Pontius Pilate meet together with the Gentiles and the people of Israel? Why did they conspire against Jesus? It was because God had decided beforehand that this is what should happen. Christ's death was a necessity. God was so in control of events that everything took place exactly as he had planned.

You realize that if that was true for Jesus, then it is also true for you. Everything that happens in your life must happen as it does. It is part of God's plan. That you were born when you were, to whom you were, where you were; that your life has taken the direction it has; that you are doing the kind of work you do; that you have married whom you have—everything has taken place according to God's plan. It was necessary that all these things happen.

### Yet there was free choice

But wait a minute? Does that mean I have no choice? Am I just a puppet on a string, forced to move and act only as God pulls the strings? No. No more so than Christ was a puppet.

The Son of God freely chose to come into this world as a human being. Jesus willingly went to Jerusalem, knowing full well what awaited him there. Jesus allowed himself to be arrested, to be nailed to a cross, and to die. All this was contingent on what Jesus thought and did. From the viewpoint of contingency it came about by free choice.

Judas Iscariot was not forced to betray Jesus into the hands of his enemies. Even at the last, Jesus warned Judas and made it clear that Judas was doing this by his own decision. As they sat at the table in the upper room, Jesus said, "The hand of him who is going to betray me is with mine on the table. The Son of Man will go as it has been decreed, but woe to that man who betrays him" (Luke 22:21,22). Nobody was forcing Judas to do it. He could have backed out at any time.

The Jews were not forced to shout "Crucify! Crucify!" (John 19:6) or to say to Pilate, "If you let this man go, you are no friend of Caesar. Anyone who claims to be a king opposes Caesar" (verse 12) or to say, "Take him away! Take him away! Crucify him!" (verse 15). The Jews freely chose to say these things. Jesus' death was contingent on their handing him over to Pilate and calling for his crucifixion.

Pontius Pilate was not forced to pronounce the death sentence on Jesus. Pilate knew Jesus was innocent. He said, "I find no basis for a charge against him" (verse 6). Right then he could have let Jesus go. He had the power to do so, and in fact, he did try to set Jesus free, but when the Jews kept shouting, "If you let this man go, you are no friend of Caesar" (verse 12), Pilate decided to hand Jesus over to be crucified. He wasn't forced to do it; he did it freely. Jesus' death was contingent on Pilate's issuance of the order of crucifixion.

You realize what you do makes a difference too. Your going to the store, for example, is dependent on free choices you make. You decide there are some groceries you need to pick up. You make a list. You get into your car. You drive your car to the store. You purchase the groceries. You bring them back home. All these things happen because you have freely chosen to do them. Your getting groceries is contingent on what you do. It doesn't have to happen when it does, how it does, the way it does, and you probably don't have to buy all those extra snack foods either! Nobody is forcing you to do it. You simply decide to do it.

### Bound to means

Because things don't necessarily have to happen the way they do, we are bound to use the means God has provided for our welfare. This is extremely practical for daily life. We could say that if God intends for us to survive, he'll cause it to happen regardless of what we do, but that would be foolish because our survival depends on what we do.

On his way to Rome for trial before Caesar, Paul was on a ship caught in a terrible storm. For 14 days the ship had been tossed about by the wind and waves. For all that time the men on board the ship had gone without food. They were terrified, and possibly some were seasick. Paul said to them, "I urge you to take some food. You need it to survive" (Acts 27:34). A person can go without food for only so long. God doesn't intend for us to abstain from food. God created food to be "received with thanksgiving" (1 Timothy 4:4).

Making a living, providing for ourselves and our families, is contingent on our working. Repeatedly the book of Proverbs commends industriousness: "Go to the ant, you sluggard; consider its ways and be wise!" (6:6). "He who works his land will have abundant food, but he who chases fantasies lacks judgment" (12:11). "Do not love sleep or you will grow poor; stay awake and you will have food to spare" (20:13). The wife of noble character is described as one who "selects wool and flax and works with eager hands" (31:13). "She sets about her work vigorously; her arms are strong for her tasks" (verse 17).

The apostle Paul worked hard as a tentmaker to provide for himself because he didn't want to be a burden to anyone. Regularly he admonished others to work too. "He who has been stealing must steal no longer, but must work, doing something useful with his own hands, that he may have something to share with those in need" (Ephesians 4:28). Regarding those in Thessalonica who were standing about idle, who were not busy but were busybodies, Paul said, "Such people we command and urge in the Lord

Jesus Christ to settle down and earn the bread they eat"
(2 Thessalonians 3:12).

To quit my job and expect God to provide for me is not
only foolish, it's wrong. My safety and well-being depend
on what I do too. I need to avoid danger. I need to stay
away from things that might hurt me. I need to be careful
not to do anything foolish.

Once the devil took Jesus to Jerusalem and had him
stand on the highest point of the temple. "'If you are the
Son of God,' he said, 'throw yourself down. For it is written: "He will command his angels concerning you, and
they will lift you up in their hands, so that you will not
strike your foot against a stone."' Jesus answered him, 'It is
also written: "Do not put the Lord your God to the test"'"
(Matthew 4:6,7). Because his personal safety was dependent on what he did, Jesus refused to jump from the highest
point of the temple. So today our personal safety is contingent on what we do. To jump off a skyscraper without a
parachute or a safety net below would be wrong. To drive
recklessly or to use power tools carelessly would be foolish.

After his conversion Saul (later called Paul) preached
in the synagogues of Damascus. He baffled the Jews as he
proved that Jesus is the Son of God and the Christ, and so
they conspired to kill him. Saul could have said, "Well, I
guess I'll just have to stay here and take my chances and
hope everything works out all right." He could have said,
"If I leave the city, they might think I'm a coward, so I'd
better stay." But Saul realized that discretion was the better part of valor. Realizing that the Jews were keeping a
close watch on the city gates in order to kill him, Saul
arranged to flee from Damascus in the middle of the night
by being lowered in a basket through an opening in the
city wall (Acts 9:25).

### In sickness

Because of contingency we are bound to the means God has provided for our welfare. This is true also in times of sickness or injury. After the conversion of Matthew, Jesus went to Matthew's house and ate with tax collectors and sinners. When the Pharisees saw this, they asked Jesus' disciples, "Why does your teacher eat with tax collectors and 'sinners'?" (Matthew 9:11). On hearing this, Jesus said, "It is not the healthy who need a doctor, but the sick" (verse 12). Jesus was speaking about spiritual sickness, but it's evident that when people were physically sick, it was assumed to be a normal thing for them to go to the doctor.

Paul's traveling companion Luke was a doctor, and no doubt, Paul had many occasions to turn to his physician friend for treatment after beatings and stonings or maybe even for relief of sore muscles and feet after miles and miles of walking.

When we are seriously ill, we need to go to a doctor. We need to take seriously the remedies our doctor suggests.

Although Isaiah was not a doctor, his remedy for King Hezekiah was followed, and it worked. "Isaiah said, 'Prepare a poultice of figs.' They did so and applied it to the boil, and he [King Hezekiah] recovered" (2 Kings 20:7). Isaiah once said to Judah and Jerusalem, "From the sole of your foot to the top of your head there is no soundness—only wounds and welts and open sores, not cleansed or bandaged or soothed with oil" (Isaiah 1:6). Though Isaiah is speaking symbolically about Judah and Jerusalem's spiritual corruption, his words do suggest something about the importance of using remedies for wounds.

You recall Jesus' story about the good Samaritan, who, when he found the man who had been beaten and left half dead, "went to him and bandaged his wounds, pouring on oil and wine" (Luke 10:34). Those were first-century remedies doctors would prescribe.

Timothy, who had stomach problems and suffered from frequent illnesses, was told by Paul, "Stop drinking only water, and use a little wine" (1 Timothy 5:23). That too was a first-century remedy.

If anyone in the congregation was sick, James said, "He should call the elders of the church to pray over him and anoint him with oil in the name of the Lord" (5:14). In those days that was perhaps tantamount to telling somebody to take a couple of aspirin, drink plenty of liquids, and get some bed rest.

The Bible often speaks about medical remedies. If a person breaks a bone, he needs to have it set and have his arm or leg put in a cast (Ezekiel 30:21). If people have a contagious disease, they need to be placed under quarantine (Leviticus 13:4). From such examples, it is clear that when we are sick or wounded or injured, the Lord expects us to use whatever means he has provided for us to recover and be healthy again.

The Christian Scientist who refuses all medical treatment as a matter of principle is clearly going contrary to God's will. It is not an indication of lack of faith to turn to doctors and medicine. Rather, it is what God expects us to do. Our health is contingent on our doing that.

Of course, we need to remember that we not only turn to medicine and doctors, but also to the Lord in prayer. King Asa of Judah was afflicted with a disease in his feet. The Bible says that, "though his disease was severe, even in his illness he did not seek help from the LORD, but only from the physicians" (2 Chronicles 16:12). It was proper for Asa to go to the physicians, but improper for him not also to seek help from the Lord.

### The means of grace

Using the means God has given also applies to our spiritual sickness. God has provided certain means for our spiritual welfare. To fail to use these may prove to be disastrous—eternally disastrous.

Because all people are descendants of Adam and Eve, they share their guilt, have inherited the corruption that leads to actual sins, and are under God's wrath by nature. In Baptism God applies to us all the blessings of Christ's redemption. By the washing of water and the Word we are cleansed from sin and become God's dear children and heirs of heaven. That is why Jesus instructed his disciples in what we call the Great Commission to "go and make disciples of all nations, baptizing them in the name of the Father and of the Son and of the Holy Spirit" (Matthew 28:19). Baptism is something essential, something vital. That's why Jesus said, "Whoever believes and is baptized will be saved" (Mark 16:16) and why he said to Nicodemus, who came to him by night, "I tell you the truth, no one can enter the kingdom of God unless he is born of water and the Spirit" (John 3:5). On Pentecost as Peter preached to the large crowd of people in Jerusalem, he said, "Repent and be baptized, every one of you, in the name of Jesus Christ for the forgiveness of your sins" (Acts 2:38).

A person might say, "I'm not going to baptize my children. I'd rather wait until they're old enough to understand and let them decide for themselves whether they want to be baptized." That would be foolish and wrong. Baptism is a means whereby God brings little children into his kingdom. Their entrance into the kingdom is contingent on their being baptized.

Because the gospel is the means whereby God creates and strengthens faith, we need to hear it. "Faith comes from hearing the message, and the message is heard through the word of Christ" (Romans 10:17). We cannot say, "I have heard the gospel, and I believe in Jesus, so there really is no need for me to continue to hear or read or study that message. I already know it." That is just as foolish as saying, "I ate once last year, and so I don't need ever to eat again." Just as our bodies continually need nourishment to stay healthy and to remain alive, so our souls regularly need spiritual nourishment to stay healthy and alive.

Jesus' parable of the sower teaches that regular, fruitful hearing of the Word is absolutely necessary. In explaining the parable to his disciples, Jesus says, "The one who received the seed that fell on good soil is the man who hears the word and understands it. He produces a crop, yielding a hundred, sixty or thirty times what was sown" (Matthew 13:23).

While Martha was distracted by all the preparations that had to be made for her dinner for Jesus, her sister, Mary, sat at Jesus' feet listening to what he said. When Martha complained that Mary wasn't helping, Jesus said, "Only one thing is needed. Mary has chosen what is better, and it will not be taken away from her" (Luke 10:42).

One purpose for which Jesus fed the five thousand with five small barley loaves and two small fish was that he wanted to teach his disciples an important lesson about hearing his Word and believing in him. Jesus said, "I am the living bread that came down from heaven. If anyone eats of this bread, he will live forever. This bread is my flesh, which I will give for the life of the world" (John 6:51). Just as we need regularly to eat bread, so we need to partake of Jesus, the living Bread. We need to hear his Word and believe it for our faith to be nurtured and strengthened.

On Pentecost the disciples not only baptized people, but Peter proclaimed the gospel message. It was important that the people hear—and continue to hear—that message so their faith could grow.

Luke speaks favorably of the new Christians in Berea because they were not content simply to have heard the gospel once but "received the message with great eagerness and examined the Scriptures every day to see if what Paul said was true" (Acts 17:11). To the Christians in Thessalonica Paul said that the gospel, which Paul and his companions had preached to them, was "the word of God, which is at work in you who believe" (1 Thessalonians 2:13). The apostle Peter admonishes his readers, "Like newborn babies, crave pure spiritual milk, so that by it you may grow up in your salvation, now that you have tasted that the Lord is good" (1 Peter 2:2,3). Just as babies need milk to grow and be strong, so we all need pure spiritual milk, the gospel message, so that we might grow up in our salvation.

Holy Communion is also a means whereby the Lord strengthens our faith. Because of contingency, we are bound to use that means of grace regularly and often. In instituting this Holy Supper Jesus said, "Take and eat; this is my body. . . . Drink from it, all of you. This is my blood of the covenant, which is poured out for many for the forgiveness of sins" (Matthew 26:26-28). Jesus also said, "Do this in remembrance of me" (Luke 22:19). Concerning the Lord's Supper Paul said, "Whenever you eat this bread and drink this cup, you proclaim the Lord's death until he comes" (1 Corinthians 11:26).

When we realize what the Lord does for us in this wonderful Supper, how could we ever turn our backs on it and walk away? We need this food for our souls even more than we need food for our bodies. Our spiritual welfare is dependent on using the means of grace, just as our physical welfare is dependent on using the means God has given.

### The dangers of denying necessity and contingency

Back to our original question. Does everything have to happen the way it does, or could things happen otherwise? The scriptural answer to that question is yes. Both parts of the question are true.

To deny necessity, to say that things do not have to happen the way they do, is tantamount to saying that there is no God and adopting the philosophy of Epicureanism, which says that in a world without God there can be no purpose or design, no final or absolute good, and so the highest good is pleasure.

Could things happen otherwise? We might sometimes think we're being particularly religious and pious if we say that everything has to happen the way it does. But to deny that things could happen otherwise is tantamount to fatalism and Stoicism, and these ideas have nothing more to do with Christianity than does Epicureanism.

The Bible teaches both necessity and contingency. It teaches that from God's point of view everything must happen the way it does, and it teaches that from our human point of view things could happen otherwise. This does not satisfy our human logic, but this is the truth, and this is what we believe.

# 7

# What about the End of Life?

"It doesn't much matter what you do. When your number's up, it's up." You wonder if those who say such things have a point. You've heard about people who didn't exercise, didn't take care of themselves, didn't watch their diet and yet lived to a ripe old age. You've also heard about people who were supposedly in excellent health, took good care of themselves, jogged, exercised, were careful about their diet but yet died young.

You've tried to watch your diet, but you find yourself somewhat overweight. You've tried dieting a number of times, but there's always so much good food, and you're often very hungry. Does it really make any difference? "When your number's up, it's up."

Does it really matter if you watch your sodium intake and the cholesterol and fat content of foods? You've been careful to read the labels on the products you buy at the grocery store. You've been fairly conscious about what you eat. You've tried to follow the food-pyramid guidelines, eating plenty of carbohydrates, fruits, and vegetables and taking it easy on meat, sweets, and fried foods, but you wonder if it really makes any difference. "When your number's up, it's up."

You've tried all sorts of ways to get regular exercise over the years. You've purchased an exercise bicycle, rowing machine, set of weights, trampoline, and skiing machine, and from time to time you've been diligent in using them, but then you got busy with something else or lost interest, and you gave it up. Now you're wondering if it really made that much difference anyway. You tried jogging for a while but discovered that wasn't for you. You bought a swimming pass at the local pool but discovered that the times for lap swim didn't always fit into your schedule, and you became busy with other things. Lately you've been going for a brisk walk as often as you can, but you're wondering if any of this makes that much difference. "When your number's up, it's up."

You gave up smoking years ago because you thought it was the right thing to do, but you know people who smoke and seem to be perfectly healthy. You know of people who have a daily cocktail, and it doesn't seem to have a negative effect on them. In fact, every so often you hear of a study that says having an occasional cocktail is good for a person, and you wonder if it's true or if someone's just trying to rationalize that lifestyle.

You wonder, "Does what I do really make a difference as far as the length of my life is concerned?"

## God has determined the end of life

The Bible makes it clear that God has determined the end of each human life. Job says to the Lord, "Man's days are determined; you have decreed the number of his months and have set limits he cannot exceed" (14:5). From the viewpoint of necessity we must say that the length of our lives has been absolutely determined by God down to the very number of years, months, days, and hours. God has determined "when our number is up," and nothing we do can change that.

King David said to the Lord, "All the days ordained for me were written in your book before one of them came to be" (Psalm 139:16). In the preceding verses David speaks about how God created his inmost being and knit him together in his mother's womb, how his frame was not hidden from God when God made him in the secret place, when he was woven together in the depths of the earth. From the very beginning of David's life God had determined exactly how many days he would live in this world. Even before he was born, it was all written down in God's book. God had decided. It was not going to change. So it would be.

As Paul spoke to the philosophers in Athens, he prepared the way for the gospel of Jesus by sharing thoughts about God that they should have known from their natural knowledge of God. He reminded them that the God who made the world and everything in it does not live in temples made by human hands and does not need to be served by human beings, because he is the one who gives all people life and breath and everything else. And then Paul said, "From one man he made every nation of men, that they should inhabit the whole earth; and he determined the times set for them and the exact places where they should live" (Acts 17:26). God is the origin of human life. God created every human being who has ever lived, and he has determined for each of the billions upon billions of people in the world the exact places where they will live and the exact amount of time they will live.

Once a man from the crowd asked Jesus to make his brother give him his share of an inheritance. In response Jesus warned the crowd about greed and then told a parable to illustrate that life does not consist in having possessions. A certain rich man had had a particularly abundant crop one year, so much that he didn't have room to store it all. So he decided to tear down his barns and build bigger ones. He said to himself, "You have plenty of good things laid up for many years. Take life easy; eat, drink and be merry" (Luke 12:19). But that night God said to him, "You fool! This very night your life will be demanded from you" (verse 20). Jesus was warning about the sin of greed and about setting hearts on earthly things, but he was also teaching that God determines the length of a person's life. Just when a person thinks he or she has plenty of time to enjoy life, God may cut his or her life short.

When Mary and Joseph brought Jesus to the temple in Jerusalem to present him to the Lord in keeping with the law of the Lord, they met a man there named Simeon, who was waiting for the fulfillment of God's promise of a Savior. God had revealed to Simeon that he "would not die before he had seen the Lord's Christ" (Luke 2:26). God had determined the length of Simeon's life, and no matter how old he was, no matter what he thought, no matter what others thought about when he would die, God had decided exactly when it would be.

The apostle Paul had a desire to depart and be with his Lord in heaven, but he knew that would not happen until

God determined that it should. Paul was beaten, scourged, sick, hungry, thirsty—and yet he knew that no matter what happened, he would not die until God decided it was time.

God once called a man named Gideon to deliver his people from the Midianites. Gideon was reluctant to serve. He needed a sign that it really was the Lord talking to him. In response to the Angel of the Lord's instructions, Gideon placed meat and unleavened bread on a rock. When the Angel of the Lord touched the meat and bread, fire flared from the rock and consumed the meat and bread. When Gideon realized he had seen the Angel of the Lord face to face, he was terrified. "But the LORD said to him, 'Peace! Do not be afraid. You are not going to die'" (Judges 6:23). Even though he had seen the Angel of the Lord, Gideon would not die before the Lord determined it was time.

In Moses' prayer recorded in the Bible as Psalm 90, he says to the Lord, "You turn men back to dust, saying, 'Return to dust, O sons of men'" (verse 3). God, who made people from the dust of the earth, causes them to return to the dust when he determines it is the right time.

### God can prolong or shorten life

If God has determined the end of human life, how then are we to understand the promise of the Fourth Commandment: "Honor your father and your mother, so that you may live long in the land the LORD your God is giving you" (Exodus 20:12)? The same promise is found in the book of Proverbs: "My son, do not forget my teaching, but keep my commands in your heart, for they will prolong your life many years and bring you prosperity" (3:1,2). "Listen, my son, accept what I say, and the years of your life will be many" (4:10). Does God really prolong a person's life as a reward for obedience to parents? What about godly children who die young? Does God really change his mind about the length of a person's life? Yes, but only in the sense that it appears to us as if God changes his mind and prolongs or shortens a person's life. And when a godly person dies young, there may be a special reason, as we shall consider.

God sometimes prolongs life for the good of his church. Paul was certain that God would continue to deliver him from deadly perils in response to the prayers of the believers (2 Corinthians 1:10,11). Even though he was in constant danger, Paul was convinced that the Lord would permit him to live. He told the Philippians, "I know that I will remain, and I will continue with all of you for your progress and joy in the faith" (1:25). God still had work for Paul to do and so would prolong his life until that work was finished.

Scripture says that God prolongs life for his purposes, but it also teaches that God shortens life as he determines.

Sometimes God shortens the lives of the wicked as a punishment for their sins. Jacob's son Judah once married a Canaanite woman who bore him three sons. When Judah's firstborn son, Er, was grown, Judah found a wife for him named Tamar. But Er lived a wicked life, so "the LORD put him to death" (Genesis 38:7). The law of the levirate (Deuteronomy 25:5,6) said that the next oldest brother was to marry the widow to provide offspring for the dead brother, but Er's brother Onan refused to fulfill his obligation, and the Bible says, "What he did was wicked in the LORD's sight; so he put him to death also" (Genesis 38:10). God shortened the lives of both Er and Onan because of their wickedness.

Sometimes God also shortens the lives of believers. The Bible says, "The righteous are taken away to be spared from evil" (Isaiah 57:1). The Lord only knows what dreadful things might happen to a person should he or she live. To spare that person, the Lord shortens his or her life. We sometimes may wonder why a young person's life is cut short or why a child or even a baby dies. Here is part of the answer. God wants to spare that person from evil.

### Length of life and the use of means

Thus far we have considered that life ends when God determines that it should. Even though God may prolong or shorten people's lives, from the viewpoint of necessity we must say that God has determined when the end of each person's life should be.

However, the Bible also teaches that the end of life is contingent on what people do or do not do. It gives the lie to the thinking that when your number's up, it's up. The case of King Hezekiah makes this clear.

King Hezekiah of Judah became ill and was at the point of death. The prophet Isaiah went to him and told him to put his house in order because he was going to die. Hezekiah immediately turned to the Lord in prayer. The Lord's response came through the prophet Isaiah: "I have heard your prayer and seen your tears; I will add fifteen years to your life" (Isaiah 38:5). The Lord in grace and mercy extended Hezekiah's life in response to his prayer.

### We need to use the means

The Bible says that if we use the means God has given for our welfare, our lives will be extended. To remain alive, for example, we need to eat. Paul told the people on board the storm-tossed ship, "For the last fourteen days . . . you have been in constant suspense and have gone without food—you haven't eaten anything. Now I urge you to take some food. You need it to survive" (Acts 27:33,34). They had been so worried about drowning they had forgotten that if they didn't eat something, they would eventually starve to death. It is important to eat. It is necessary to be careful what we eat. We ought to eat a balanced diet and pay attention to the food pyramid. It may be very important for certain people to avoid sodium, cholesterol, fat, sweets, or dairy products. From the viewpoint of contingency the end of life is not decreed. It depends on eating—and eating properly.

Medicine and other medical treatments may be another means God uses to prolong our lives. If, for instance, we contract a life-threatening infection and an antibiotic could cure us of the infection, it would be wrong to refuse the medical treatment. Again, we see from the viewpoint of contingency that the end of life is not decreed. It may depend on making use of the blessings of medical treatment.

God promises to extend the lives of those who are obedient and pious. Shortly after Solomon had become king, the Lord appeared to him in a dream and told him, "If you walk in my ways and obey my statutes and commands as David your father did, I will give you a long life" (1 Kings 3:14). Concerning the person who loves him, acknowledges his name, and calls upon him, the Lord says, "With long life will I satisfy him and show him my salvation" (Psalm 91:16). Proverbs 10:27 says, "The fear of the LORD adds length to life." In words of instruction to his children, David says, "Whoever of you loves life and desires to see many good days, keep your tongue from evil and your lips from speaking lies. Turn from evil and do good; seek peace and pursue it" (Psalm 34:12-14).

For a person to continue to live, it is also necessary to avoid danger. Sometimes people have the idea that they can live dangerously, that they can do anything they want because nothing will happen to them until "their number's up." They may drive carelessly. They may take terrible risks. They may engage in death-defying activities. Such things are not only foolish, they are wrong. They tempt God. The devil wanted Jesus to cast himself down from the pinnacle of the temple, but Jesus refused to do it because that would be tempting God (Matthew 4:5-7). It would not be in accord with God's normal way of watching over people.

### Life shortened by not using the means

Just as using the means God has given will lengthen life, so not using them will shorten life. People who do not eat, use their prescribed medicines, or avoid danger will normally not live as long as those who do.

King David's son Absalom was vain, proud, and rebellious. He sought to steal the hearts of the people from his father and eventually led a rebellion against him. It proved his undoing. As he was riding his mule under the thick branches of a large oak tree, Absalom's head got caught in the tree, and he was left hanging in midair. When David's general, Joab, and his men found Absalom, they put him to death (2 Samuel 18:9-15). A wicked life may be a very short life.

One of David's advisers, a man named Ahithophel, had gone over to Absalom's side. When Ahithophel saw that his advice was not being followed, he went and hanged himself (2 Samuel 17:23). Those who commit suicide shorten their lives by their own evil action.

Those who commit murder may face the death penalty. God said to Noah after the flood, "Whoever sheds the blood of man, by man shall his blood be shed; for in the image of God has God made man" (Genesis 9:6). God may also shorten the lives of the wicked.

God has determined exactly how long each person will live. He may prolong or shorten a life as he sees fit, but always a person dies when God decides that he or she should. On the other hand, we must say that what we do makes a difference. God has given us certain means to extend our lives and improve the quality of our lives, and using those means will do just that. To our minds it's a contradiction, nevertheless both parts of the equation— God's providence and our responsibility—are true, and that leads us to say once again, "If God cares, then so should we."

# 8

# Problems Connected with Providence

You know you're not alone in wondering if God is all powerful, if God can do anything, why doesn't he just destroy evil? God created all things in heaven and on earth, visible and invisible—why did he create angels he knew would fall away from him and bring evil into his good creation? God is holy, righteous, and good. How could he allow this to happen? If God preserves his creation and everything in it today, why didn't he preserve it from evil to begin with? If God protects all people and all creatures today, why didn't he protect them from the possibility of evil from the very beginning?

### The origin and cause of evil

The Bible does not permit the possibility that God in any way is the origin or the cause of evil. Jesus once told a story about a man who sowed good seed in his field, but while everyone was sleeping, his enemy came and sowed weeds among the wheat. When the crowd left, Jesus explained the parable to his disciples. He said, "The one who sowed the good seed is the Son of Man. The field is the world, and the good seed stands for the sons of the kingdom. The weeds are the sons of the evil one, and the enemy who sows them is the devil" (Matthew 13:37-39). Clearly, the devil is responsible for evil, unbelief, and wickedness. But why doesn't God stop him?

There is a great deal of evil around us in the world. Jesus warned his disciples, "Be careful, or your hearts will be weighed down with dissipation, drunkenness and the anxieties of life" (Luke 21:34). James warned his readers that "friendship with the world is hatred toward God" and that "anyone who chooses to be a friend of the world becomes an enemy of God" (4:4). The apostle Paul warned the Romans, "Do not conform any longer to the pattern of this world" (12:2). John writes, "Do not love the world or anything in the world" (1 John 2:15). Paul reminds the Ephesians that they were dead in transgressions and sins when they "followed the ways of this world" (2:2). If God is all-powerful, why doesn't he protect his people from the evil in the world? Why doesn't he preserve us from sin, corruption, and wickedness?

The Bible says, "The hearts of men . . . are full of evil and there is madness in their hearts while they live" (Ecclesiastes 9:3). Through the prophet Jeremiah the Lord says, "The heart is deceitful above all things and beyond cure" (Jeremiah 17:9). Jesus once said, "From within, out of men's hearts, come evil thoughts, sexual immorality, theft, murder, adultery, greed, malice, deceit, lewdness, envy, slander, arrogance and folly" (Mark

7:21,22). If God is all-powerful, why doesn't he preserve us from the evil welling up inside us? Why doesn't he protect us from ourselves?

All these are questions the Bible doesn't answer specifically. It does tell us that the origin of evil is the devil. It tells us that the present cause of evil is the devil, the unbelieving world, and our sinful flesh. As to why God didn't preserve his creation from sin to begin with, as to why he doesn't just prevent all evil temptations from ever coming to his people, the Bible doesn't give an answer.

But the Bible does clearly tell us what God did. God provided the complete and perfect solution to evil by sending his Son into the world. Jesus came into this world to defeat all our enemies. The letter to the Hebrews says, "Since the children have flesh and blood, he [the Son of God] too shared in their humanity so that by his death he might destroy him who holds the power of death—that is, the devil" (2:14). In his first epistle John writes, "The reason the Son of God appeared was to destroy the devil's work" (3:8).

Even before he created the world, God had in mind what he would do to rescue the world. The Bible says, "This grace was given us in Christ Jesus before the beginning of time, but it has now been revealed through the appearing of our Savior, Christ Jesus, who has destroyed death and has brought life and immortality to light through the gospel" (2 Timothy 1:9,10). By his death Christ destroyed the power of death. It no longer can hold us. His resurrection guarantees our resurrection from the dead to life eternal in heaven. Christ's work of redemption has overcome the guilt of our sin, which would have condemned us to hell. "There is now no condemnation for those who are in Christ Jesus" (Romans 8:1).

Christ's work of redemption has also overcome the power of sin in our lives. Writing to Titus, Paul says, "We wait for the blessed hope—the glorious appearing of our great God and Savior, Jesus Christ, who gave himself for us to redeem us from all wickedness and to purify for himself a people that are his very own, eager to do what is good" (2:13,14). Though there are questions that we cannot answer about the origin of evil and the present existence of evil, in the gospel we have the answer we need. God did provide a solution. In our daily lives we have the victory over sin, death, and the devil as we live by faith in Christ Jesus.

### Free will

From what the Bible teaches about contingency, it is clear that in earthly matters we freely make decisions and that things happen differently as a consequence of our decisions. We are not puppets controlled by a master puppeteer in the heavens. We are not complex robots programmed by God to act and behave in a certain way. We are free, self-determining beings. We have a free will in earthly matters.

But we are not born with a free will in spiritual matters. By nature we are slaves to sin and can do nothing but sin; we have no choice. By our own power, we are not capable of making any decision that is good, right, or holy. According to our sinful nature, we are prisoners of the law of sin at work within the members of our bodies (Romans 7:23). We were born captives of the devil, bound to do his will (2 Timothy 2:26). It is only in Christ and the gospel that we are truly free. Paul says, "Through Christ Jesus the law of the Spirit of life set me free from the law of sin and death" (Romans 8:2). Made new in Christ, we are no longer slaves to sin and the devil. Now, according to the new man, we freely and gladly serve our Lord as we live under the freedom of the gospel (Ephesians 4:24). To the Corinthians Paul says, "Where the Spirit of the Lord is, there is freedom" (2 Corinthians 3:17). Now we are truly free—free to do the Lord's will, free to do those things that please him, free to serve others.

### God's providence and decisions

Decisions, decisions. It seems you constantly have to make decisions. You have to decide what time to set the alarm to get up in the morning. You need to decide what to wear. You must decide what to have for breakfast, whether to have a big, nutritious breakfast or simply a piece of toast and a cup of coffee. You need to decide what you will do during the day, what projects you will try to accomplish around the house, what you will do at work, whether you will call a friend or contact a relative, whether you will live dangerously or play it safe. Life is full of decisions.

What does God's providence have to do with the decisions you make every day? Is God providing for you regardless of what you decide to do? Is he protecting you no matter what choices you make?

As the Israelites were about to cross the Jordan to possess the land, Moses delivered a farewell address. He commanded them to love the Lord their God, to walk in his ways, and to keep his laws. If they did that, Moses said, they would live and increase in property and number. The Lord would bless them in the land they were about to possess. But if they chose to turn away from the Lord, if they bowed down to other gods to worship them, Moses told them they would certainly be destroyed. They would not live long in the land they were about to enter. Moses said, "I have set before you life and death, blessings and curses. Now choose life, so that you and your children may live and that you may love the LORD your God, listen to his voice, and hold fast to him. For the LORD is your life, and he will give you many years in the land he swore to give to your fathers, Abraham, Isaac and Jacob" (Deuteronomy 30:19,20). But what about those Israelites who chose not to follow the Lord? Did God provide for them? Did he protect them?

In the covenant renewal ceremony at Shechem, Joshua challenged the Israelites to fear the Lord and serve him with all faithfulness, to throw away the gods their forefathers had worshiped in Mesopotamia and Egypt and serve the Lord only. Joshua said, "If serving the LORD seems undesirable to you, then choose for yourselves this day whom you will serve. . . . But as for me and my household, we will serve the LORD" (Joshua 24:15). Would the Lord preserve and watch over only Joshua, his household, and the others who remained faithful to him? What about those who forsook the Lord to serve other gods? Did the Lord not provide for them?

Naomi and her daughters-in-law, Orpah and Ruth, had become widows in the land of Moab. When Naomi heard that the Lord had provided food for his people in Judah, she decided to return to her home country. Orpah and Ruth said they wanted to go with Naomi. But Naomi discouraged them and told them to stay in Moab. That is what Orpah decided to do. But Ruth said to Naomi, "Don't urge me to leave you or to turn back from you. Where you go I will go, and where you stay I will stay. Your people will be my people and your God my God" (Ruth 1:16). We know that the Lord provided for Naomi and Ruth in the land of

Judah. Ruth gleaned in the fields and was thereby able to provide grain for herself and her mother-in-law. The Lord also provided Boaz as her new husband. But what about Orpah? Did the Lord not provide for her because she chose to stay in Moab? Is God's provision and preservation determined by the decisions people make?

Following the lead of his wicked wife, Jezebel, King Ahab of Israel permitted the worship of Baal and Asherah in the land of Israel. When the Lord's prophet Elijah called on people to turn from these idols to the true God, Ahab accused Elijah of bringing trouble to Israel. Elijah responded that Ahab was the actual cause of Israel's troubles because he had abandoned the Lord and followed the baals. And then Elijah invited Ahab to summon the Israelites and bring all the prophets of Baal and Asherah to meet him on Mount Carmel. Elijah stepped before the people there and said, "How long will you waver between two opinions? If the LORD is God, follow him; but if Baal is God, follow him" (1 Kings 18:21). Would a decision to follow Baal cut them off from God's providential care? Were Ahab and Jezebel no longer under God's protection? Does the Lord provide only for those who follow him and make decisions that are pleasing to him?

In answering these questions, we notice that Scripture speaks of what we might call different degrees of God's providence. Jesus clearly says that his heavenly Father "causes his sun to rise on the evil and the good, and sends rain on the righteous and the unrighteous" (Matthew 5:45). While all people, believers and unbelievers alike, benefit from God's providential care, Scripture also makes it clear that the Lord singles out his believing children as the special objects of his love. Psalm 145:17-20 makes this distinction: "The LORD is righteous in all his ways and loving toward all he has made. The LORD is near to all who call on him, to all who call on him in truth. He fulfills the desires of those who fear him; he hears their cry and saves them. The LORD watches over all who love him, but all the wicked he will destroy." Only believers have God's promise to hear and answer their prayers as he guides their lives. Only believers have God's promise to send his angels to guard them in all their ways (Psalm 91:11; Hebrews 1:14). Only believers have God's promise to make all things, even bad things, serve their good (Romans 8:28).

God certainly provides for all, especially for his believers. He can and often does overrule our bad decisions and doesn't always let us suffer the consequences. In his wisdom and disciplinary love, the Lord sometimes also lets believers suffer some of the temporal consequences of their bad decisions. God did not let Moses live long enough to enter the Promised Land as a direct consequence of the bad decision he made at Kadesh (Numbers 20:1-12). Paul told the Christians in Corinth that the reason some of them had fallen sick and died was because of the way they had abused God's gift of Holy Communion (1 Corinthians 11:28-32).

As believers we recognize God's love as he provides and cares for all people, especially his believers. As believers we also recognize that in Jesus, God's saving love provided the Savior we all need to rescue us from the eternal consequences of our sins and all the bad decisions we have ever made. Recognizing the greatness especially of God's saving love, we will want to be careful always to seek the Lord's guidance so that we make good decisions.

# 9

## Incorrect Views about Providence

You have learned many comforting things about God's providence as it is taught in the Bible. As you mull those truths over in your mind, you realize that others have held to beliefs about providence that contradict what the Bible teaches. Basically, these false teachings can be divided into two groups: those that deny contingency (Stoicism, determinism, fatalism) and those that deny necessity (Epicureanism, Deism). We begin this chapter by briefly examining these false views.

### Stoicism

Stoicism was founded by a man named Zeno (340–265 B.C.), who taught that the universe was controlled by an

absolute reason or divine will and that everything that
happened was determined not by chance but by a progres-
sive purpose. The Stoics believed that nature was the way
it should be and that whatever happened was regulated by
providence. It was impossible to alter the process or prevent the inevitable course of things, they said. The universe and everything that happened simply had to be
accepted. It could not be changed.

According to the Stoics, God took no interest in people
because he was not personal. The Stoics believed man's
only function was to bring his will into harmony with
whatever happened. Practical wisdom, bravery, justice,
self-control, and not being bound to things or to life
itself—these things characterized the Stoics.

Stoicism seems to make sense and appears in some
ways akin to Christianity. But Stoic and Christian ethics
are mutually exclusive. Stoicism says we are helpless
pawns controlled by fate rather than free, self-determining beings. Stoicism thus denies what the Bible teaches
about contingency.

### Determinism

Similar to Stoicism, determinism is the theory that
everything is absolutely determined by higher powers and
causes. John Calvin, whose doctrinal system is confessed
by many Reformed churches, was a theological deter-
minist. He believed that God had elected some to be
saved and others to be lost. He taught that Jesus died
only for those who were elected to salvation and that
when the gospel comes to those people, they cannot
resist it. Since God has determined that they shall be
saved, they will persevere in the faith regardless of what
happens. In all things Calvin stressed the sovereignty of

God. God is in control, he said. God determines every-thing that happens.

Materialism is a mechanical determinism that regards matter as the original cause of all things, even psychic phenomena. It asserts that even psychic processes are due to changes in material molecules, and therefore it denies the existence of God and the soul. Materialism says there is no higher power. What we see and what we are is all there is.

Economic determinism, part of the belief of Karl Marx, is the philosophy which holds that the economy of any society determines the course of its social, political, and intellectual development.

Whether the cause is theological, mechanical, or eco-nomic, determinism holds that everything is absolutely determined. There is nothing anyone can do about it. Like Stoicism, determinism thus denies what the Bible teaches about contingency.

### Fatalism

Related to determinism is fatalism. Fatalism is the idea that all things are fixed in advance for all time in such a way that human beings are powerless to change them. In classical mythology the Fates were thought to be three goddesses who determined the course of human life. The ancient Greeks believed that not even the great gods on Mount Olympus could change things if the Fates had decided otherwise. Fatalism denies the possibility of any kind of personal relationship between a person and God and leads to pessimism, the view that regards life in this world as the worst possible existence and man's lot as hopeless.

Fatalism is a prominent feature of Islam. The very word *Islam* means "submission" and emphasizes that a person is to submit to Allah. Allah absolutely controls everything, so the only thing to do is submit to his will.

Stoicism, determinism, and fatalism may vary from one another in the details, but all of them deny what the Bible teaches about contingency, man's responsibility under God.

### Epicureanism

The Epicurean, on the other hand, denies what the Bible says about necessity because he believes only two things in this world are certain and enduring—atoms and void. From the chance combination of atoms everything else comes into being, the Epicurean says. When a person dies, the body's atoms enter the void and begin a slow dissolution so that after death there is no life or consciousness. According to the Epicurean, a person's proper concern is with this life only, and pleasure is the greatest good and the sole aim of existence.

The Epicureans in the ancient world did not understand pleasure in the crass sense but as a peaceful, independent state of body and mind free from pain and trouble. They wished to free people from the fears that rob them of happiness: death, the fear of gods, and the fear of mysterious powers in nature. Since they believed there really is no god to whom people are responsible, people may do whatever they wish. Since no higher power is in control, what a person does alone determines whether he or she is going to be happy or not.

One can understand why the Epicurean philosophy has appealed to people over the years. Like Stoicism it seems to make sense. But it is a total denial of everything the

Bible teaches about God and providence. Epicureanism eventually led to hedonism, the idea that since we are masters of our own fates and are not responsible to any higher being, we might as well eat, drink, and be merry for tomorrow we die.

### Deism

Deism also has incorrect views regarding God's providence. Deism is a belief system which holds either that the universe is a self-sustaining mechanism from which God withdrew after he created it or that God is still active in the universe but only through the laws of nature. The Deist's conception of God is as a master mechanic who created the world and then left it to operate on its own. Though Deism is generally considered to have ended with Thomas Jefferson in the early 19th century, it lives on wherever a person holds to its incorrect view concerning God. A God who is absent from his creation is not providing for it. To think of God as providing for his creation simply through the laws of nature may seem logical and is even true in part, but it does not tell the whole story.

### Discerning God's will

What about attempting to discern God's will concerning some activity or endeavor about which Scripture does not directly speak? Is it possible to do that? Is it proper to do that?

Occasionally one hears a story like the following. A man had a reserved seat on an airline flight, but at the last minute he decided to cancel. Then the plane on which he would have been flying crashed, and all the people on board perished. Were his feelings God's way of revealing to him what was about to happen? Is it possible for a person to sense impending disaster? Is there such a thing as intuition? Does God operate in this way?

What about asking for signs from God whether or not to pursue a certain course of action? Gideon asked for two signs that the Lord would save Israel by his hand. If there was dew on the fleece and the ground was dry, he told the Lord that he would know he was to be the leader. When that happened, Gideon asked that the fleece would be dry and the ground covered with dew. That happened too (Judges 6:36-40).

Through the prophet Isaiah, the Lord gave King Hezekiah a sign that he would heal him. Hezekiah could ask for the sun's shadow to go forward or backward ten steps. When Hezekiah asked that the sundial go back ten steps, it happened (2 Kings 20:8-11).

While sitting in a garden, the church father Augustine (A.D. 354–430) suddenly heard the voice of a child repeating the words "Take it and read it. Take it and read it." Augustine interpreted this as a divine command to open a Bible and read the first passage on which his finger rested. Having done this, he felt that the passage he read was God's special message to him for his life.

What about reading the horoscope in the daily paper? What about the message inside a fortune cookie? Could God possibly be speaking to people through these means? Is it all right to take these things seriously?

Is it proper to have a fortune-teller look into a crystal ball, read a person's palm, study tea leaves in a cup, or look at tarot cards to try to determine what will happen? Didn't the witch of Endor conjure up Samuel, who had a message for King Saul (1 Samuel 28:3-19)? What about people who claim to have the gift of prophecy? What about people who can sense, by coming into contact with an item belonging to an individual, what is going to happen to that person?

Although God in the past has given people signs to indicate what he intends to do, he has not promised to do that today. He does not promise to speak to us directly and advise us what to do. He speaks to us in his Word. That's where we need to turn. There God tells us what he has done for us, what he does for us now, and what he will do for us in the future. There God tells us about his will for our lives. There he assures us he will watch over us, protect us, and provide for us. But the specific details of how he does this and by what ways he does this, he does not reveal, nor does he encourage us to try to determine these things.

So we ought not look to feelings, signs, horoscopes, or fortune-tellers. In fact, God expressly forbids any attempt to determine the future by means of the occult. "Let no one be found among you who . . . practices divination or sorcery, interprets omens, engages in witchcraft, or casts spells, or who is a medium or spiritist or who consults the dead. Anyone who does these things is detestable to the LORD" (Deuteronomy 18:10-12). Rather, we need to look to God and his Word and there be assured that he is watching over us to make everything serve a good purpose for us. Rather than seeking to discern God's will about the future, it is enough simply to know that God cares for us.

When faced with making a major decision, instead of looking for signs, we may follow these four steps from Scripture: (1) eliminate all options that are sinful according to God's Word, (2) pray for guidance, (3) seek advice from Christian friends, and (4) use our natural decision-making processes to evaluate which course of action would be the best, bringing the greatest glory to God and the greatest good to others and oneself.

# 10

## But What About . . .

Granted, the Bible clearly teaches that God provides for all people, all creatures, and the entire universe. But you wonder, What does this mean in my daily life? Does God provide for me according to how strongly I believe in him? To what extent is God's care for me dependent on my love for him? If some days my faith is weaker than on other days, does that mean on those "weak faith" days God is not providing for me to the same degree he is on "strong faith" days?

### Faith-healing?

Consider the following five events in Jesus' ministry from Matthew's gospel.

A man who had leprosy approached Jesus, knelt down before him, and said, "Lord, if you are willing, you can make me clean" (8:2). Jesus touched the man, told him he was indeed willing, and then cleansed him of his leprosy.

Does being healed from some disease depend on my firm conviction that the Lord can make me clean?

A Roman centurion came to Jesus with a request that Jesus heal his servant who was paralyzed and in terrible suffering. Jesus was ready to go and heal the servant, but the centurion replied that he did not deserve to have Jesus come under his roof, that Jesus should simply say the word and his servant would be healed. When Jesus heard this, he said to those around him, "I tell you the truth, I have not found anyone in Israel with such great faith" (8:10). And then Jesus told the centurion, "Go! It will be done just as you believed it would" (verse 13).

Will God provide healing from suffering for my relatives and friends only if I have a centurion-like faith?

The daughter of a certain ruler died. The ruler came to Jesus and asked that he come and put his hand on her, for then she would surely live (9:18).

Will God provide for me and my loved ones only if my faith in his life-giving power is strong enough?

As Jesus went from raising that ruler's daughter from the dead, two blind men came to him saying, "Have mercy on us, Son of David!" (9:27). Jesus asked them if they believed he was able to do this, and they replied that they did.

Does God's providence depend on the strength of my belief that he can do what I ask him to do?

"Lord, Son of David, have mercy on me! My daughter is suffering terribly from demon-possession," said a Canaanite woman from the region of Tyre and Sidon (15:22).

When Jesus did not answer, the woman kept following, pleading, and begging until he finally granted her request.

Will God provide for me only if I am persistent enough in asking him to do so?

It may seem that the Bible is teaching faith-healing, that God provides only for those whose faith is particularly strong. But such is not the case at all. God's care for me is not dependent on anything in me. It is dependent solely on his Word and promise. It was Jesus, the object of their faith, who brought healing to the leper, the centurion's servant, the ruler's daughter, the blind men, and the Canaanite woman's daughter. I don't have to ride the roller coaster of thinking that one day God will provide for me and the next day, because my faith isn't so strong, he won't provide for me. God has promised to care for me, and he will do it.

### The future?

If God promises to care for me, then is it really necessary for me to be concerned about the future, to make any plans or provisions for tomorrow? Can't I simply say, "God will provide." Especially when I don't know what the future will bring; when I realize that I have no control over the future; when I understand that there may be no future, that the world may end in the next twinkling of an eye?

What about life insurance? Is it really necessary to make the monthly payments on a life insurance policy when I don't know whether the world will continue to exist or whether I perhaps will outlive my beneficiaries? Besides, if God decides to take me to heaven, will he not provide for those I leave behind? Is buying life insurance an example of weak faith, of lack of trust in God's ability to provide?

What about setting aside some money in a savings account—a passbook account, a certificate of deposit account, or some other such vehicle? Is it all right to save money for a child's college education, to buy a home, or to buy a new car? Should I not simply trust that God will provide the financial means to do those things when the time arrives?

Or what about investing my money, playing the stock market, or investing in stocks and bonds? Is it all right to set aside some money in a tax-sheltered annuity or an IRA account? With everything I hear about the future of social security, can I be involved in that program or should I be opposed to it for conscience reasons? Aren't these things something like gambling? Am I really trusting God to provide for me if I hope to make a "killing" on the stock market or if I trust that my investments will produce excellent returns? Is all this really trusting the Lord to provide for my future?

What about estate planning, designating certain amounts from my estate to certain individuals and charitable organizations? What about having a will drawn up? Aren't these examples of failing to trust the Lord to provide for my family, my church, and other charities? Why should I try to take the future into my own hands? These are some of the questions that come to our minds when we think about what our role is in planning for the future.

It is true that the future is unknown. The end of the world is something no one can predict. Jesus said, "No one knows about that day or hour, not even the angels in heaven, nor the Son, but only the Father" (Matthew 24:36). To his disciples Jesus said, "You also must be ready, because the Son of Man will come at an hour when you do not expect him" (Luke 12:40). The Bible speaks about the end of the world coming like a flash of lightning and a thief in the night. It speaks of the end as being near at hand.

The Bible also reminds us that we do not know what the future will bring. All our careful planning may be for naught. The book of Proverbs admonishes us, "Do not boast about tomorrow, for you do not know what a day may bring forth" (27:1). No one can predict the future. That's why the writer of Ecclesiastes says: "I saw that there is nothing better for a man than to enjoy his work, because that is his lot. For who can bring him to see what will happen after him?" (3:22). James reminds us that we have no idea what is going to happen tomorrow, and then he says: "What is your life? You are a mist that appears for a little while and then vanishes" (4:14). Since we don't know when the end will come, since we don't even know what tomorrow will bring, what sense is there in making plans? Shouldn't we simply sit back and say, "God will provide"?

A winter storm was raging. The snow was coming in blinding sheets as he fought to keep his car on the road. Underneath the drifting snow was a treacherous sheet of ice. Though he crept along at about 15 miles an hour, it was white-knuckle driving such as he had never experienced. Suddenly he saw a car coming directly at him. To avoid a collision he wrenched the steering wheel to the right, causing the car to go into a spin that took him off the edge of the road and into the ditch. The man began to pray that God would deliver him. After a half hour of waiting and praying, a motorist stopped and trudged down through the snow to ask if he was all right and see if he could call for help. But the man replied, "No, thank you. I'm waiting for God to deliver me."

That man was extremely foolish. God obviously had answered his prayer by sending a motorist to help. In a similar way, we need to take advantage of all the things the Lord gives us to provide for ourselves and our families in the future. God may someday provide for our families through the life insurance policy we take out now. God may provide a college education for our children through the money we set aside in a savings account now. God may make it possible for us to help our church and other charities through the wise investing and careful Christian planning we do today.

### Punishment and chastisement?

What about when bad things happen, when tragedy strikes? Can we really say that this is part of God's providential plan for us?

Because of a famine, Naomi and her husband had moved to the land of Moab. There Naomi's husband died. Her two sons married Moabite women, one named Orpah and the other named Ruth. After about ten years both of Naomi's sons died also. She told the women of Bethlehem, "Don't call me Naomi. . . . Call me Mara, because the Almighty has made my life very bitter. I went away full, but the LORD has brought me back empty. Why call me Naomi? The LORD has afflicted me; the Almighty has brought misfortune upon me" (Ruth 1:20,21). She no longer wished to be called Naomi, meaning "pleasant," but Mara, meaning "bitter." Where was the Lord in Naomi's life? Why didn't he permit her husband and sons to live long enough to provide for her?

Or consider Job. He was an exceedingly wealthy man who owned seven thousand sheep, three thousand camels, five hundred yoke of oxen, and five hundred donkeys and

employed a large number of servants. He also had seven
sons and three daughters (Job 1:2,3). But tragedy struck.
His oxen and donkeys were stolen. The sheep and servants
were killed by fire from the sky. His camels were swept
away by raiding parties. The house in which his children
were feasting and drinking collapsed on them, and they all
died (verses 13-19). Job said, "All was well with me, but
he [the Lord] shattered me; he seized me by the neck and
crushed me. He has made me his target" (16:12). The
Lord had provided Job with rich abundance. Why did he
take it all away? Why did he later take Job's health away?
Can we really speak of God as the provider when he takes
everything away?

Moses, who had experienced God's providential care in
the wilderness, wrote, "We are consumed by your anger
and terrified by your indignation" (Psalm 90:7). How
could God, who provided his people with manna, quail,
water, and deliverance from their enemies in the wilderness, turn his back on them and reject them?

Part of the answer is that when bad things happen to
believers, these are signs of the Father's love for them. Bad
things are part of his wise providential plan for their lives.
Solomon writes, "My son, do not despise the LORD's discipline and do not resent his rebuke, because the LORD disciplines those he loves, as a father the son he delights in"
(Proverbs 3:11,12). The Lord intends problems and troubles to draw his children closer to him in love. He permits
these things to happen because they are part of his wise
plan for those about whom he cares so dearly. Just as a gar-
dener trims and prunes a tree so it will be healthy and produce more fruit, Jesus says God "cuts off every branch in
me [Jesus] that bears no fruit, while every branch that does
bear fruit he prunes so that it will be even more fruitful"

(John 15:2). God has not withdrawn his providential care from his children. On the contrary, chastisements are part of his good plans for them.

When troubles come, we should not lose heart and think God has forsaken us. The apostle Paul suffered more hardships than the average person does, but he could say: "We do not lose heart. Though outwardly we are wasting away, yet inwardly we are being renewed day by day" (2 Corinthians 4:16). Writing from prison, not knowing when or if he would be released, Paul could say to his friends at Ephesus, "I ask you, therefore, not to be discouraged because of my sufferings for you, which are your glory" (Ephesians 3:13). Paul was confident that his sufferings were serving a good purpose, and he was not discouraged by them.

Tribulations and afflictions are often blessings in disguise. Eliphaz said to his friend Job, "Blessed is the man whom God corrects; so do not despise the discipline of the Almighty" (Job 5:17). Later Job responded to Eliphaz, "He knows the way that I take; when he has tested me, I will come forth as gold" (23:10). The apostle Paul could say, "Our light and momentary troubles are achieving for us an eternal glory that far outweighs them all" (2 Corinthians 4:17).

God's plan is to keep us on the straight and narrow way that leads to heaven. If it takes troubles to accomplish that, then he will permit them to come. The writer to the Hebrews says: "No discipline seems pleasant at the time, but painful. Later on, however, it produces a harvest of righteousness and peace for those who have been trained by it" (12:11). As God disciplines his children, he gives them the certainty of eternal glory and a feeling of peace and confidence that no matter what happens, he is in control, causing all things to serve our temporal and eternal welfare.

The Lord also intends troubles and afflictions to refine and purify our faith. Peter writes to fellow Christians who were enduring great suffering, "These [afflictions] have come so that your faith—of greater worth than gold, which perishes even though refined by fire—may be proved genuine and may result in praise, glory and honor when Jesus Christ is revealed" (1 Peter 1:7). At one point in his misery, Job realized that that was the purpose of all the troubles he had to endure. He said that the Lord "knows the way that I take; when he has tested me, I will come forth as gold" (Job 23:10). The Bible makes it clear that even bad things are part of God's providential plan for us.

### Prayer?

All this leads to another question. If God has everything planned for us, if even troubles fit into his overall plan for our lives, then what is the sense of prayer? If afflictions are part of God's plan, can we hope by prayer to change God's mind? If he has set a course for our lives, does it really pay to ask him to change it?

Prayer is not something optional for a believer. God has commanded us to pray. In the Sermon on the Mount Jesus says, "Ask and it will be given to you; seek and you will find; knock and the door will be opened to you" (Matthew 7:7). Paul encourages the Ephesians to "pray in the Spirit on all occasions with all kinds of prayers and requests" (6:18). He tells the Thessalonians, "Pray continually" (1 Thessalonians 5:17). James writes: "Is any one of you in trouble? He should pray" (5:13). And in verse 16 James affirms, "The prayer of a righteous man is powerful and effective."

God commands us to pray, and he also promises that he will answer our prayers. Through his prophet Isaiah the Lord says, "Before they call I will answer; while they are still speaking I will hear" (65:24). Jesus said to his disciples, "If you remain in me and my words remain in you, ask whatever you wish, and it will be given you" (John 15:7). David says, "The LORD will hear when I call to him" (Psalm 4:3). Again David says, "The righteous cry out, and the LORD hears them; he delivers them from all their troubles" (34:17).

The Lord gives when we ask him. We find when we seek. The door is opened when we knock. Does this mean that by prayer we are changing God's predetermined course for our lives? Do we cause God's providential care to fluctuate and change by bending his ear?

In answering that question, we first need to realize that God does not always give us that for which we pray. Sometimes he refuses our requests because they are not in accord with his will. Moses asked the Lord to show him his glory, but the Lord's answer to Moses was, "You cannot see my face, for no one may see me and live" (Exodus 33:20). The Lord struck the child born of the adultery of David with Bathsheba so that he became ill. David pleaded with the Lord for the child. He fasted and spent nights lying on the ground. But the child died because what David asked was not in accord with the Lord's will (2 Samuel 12:15-18). The apostle Paul prayed earnestly and repeatedly that his thorn in the flesh might be taken from him, but the Lord's answer was, "My grace is sufficient for you, for my power is made perfect in weakness" (2 Corinthians 12:9). It was not the Lord's will that Paul's thorn be removed. James says that a person who doubts "should not think he will receive anything from the Lord"

(1:7). James also says that some people do not receive what they ask for in prayer because they are asking with wrong motives, that they may spend what they get on their pleasures (4:3).

We need to view prayer in the light of what we have learned about necessity and contingency. From God's perspective everything does have to happen the way it does. God has a plan for our lives, and he will see that plan fulfilled. From the viewpoint of contingency, however, what we do makes a difference. Prayer does make a difference. I need firmly to trust that what I ask God to do for my good and the good of others he will do. Things will happen differently because I pray about them.

Finally, I will want to pray because I know that God cares about me and has only my best interests at heart. I will want to pray because I care about what happens to my loved ones, the church, myself, and all people. And I will want to pray because I know God will hear me and answer me according to what he knows is best for me.

# 11

## Providence: A Much-Needed Doctrine

You hadn't realized how much the Bible has to say about the doctrine of God's providence. On page after page God's providence is either referred to directly or alluded to. For example, God preserved Noah and his family at the time of the flood by means of the ark. God provided for Joseph in Egypt at the house of Potiphar, in prison, and at the court of Pharaoh. God preserved Moses' life by arranging to have him adopted by Pharaoh's daughter. God provided for Moses by his education at the court of Pharaoh and by giving him a place of safety and instruction for his future work in the land of Midian. God gave young David the victory over the giant Goliath and preserved David's life when King Saul pursued him. Again and again God preserved the life of the apostle Paul from stoning, beating, scourging, shipwreck, etc. Obviously God wants us to learn the lesson well.

### The book of Esther

There is even an entire book of the Bible that has God's providence as its main theme. Over the years some people have questioned whether or not the book of Esther should be in the Bible. The name of God does not appear in the book. There is no mention of prayer or spiritual service of any kind. But the book of Esther belongs in God's Word because of its wonderful emphasis on the doctrine of God's providence.

After the Persian King Xerxes had dethroned his queen, Vashti, because she had refused to appear before the assembled princes, a kingdom-wide search for a new queen resulted in Esther, a Jewess, being chosen. That surely happened because God was controlling events.

When Mordecai, Esther's foster-father, refused to honor Haman, a Persian official, Haman was so enraged that he decided to destroy all the Jews. Mordecai reported to Esther what Haman intended to do and told her that she had the opportunity to rescue her people. He said, "If you remain silent at this time, relief and deliverance for the Jews will arise from another place, but you and your father's family will perish. And who knows but that you have come to royal position for such a time as this?" (4:14).

Mordecai was confident that somehow the Lord would provide a solution to spare the Jews from destruction and thought he might provide this solution through Queen Esther. That's exactly what happened. Esther invited the king and Haman to attend a banquet. Meanwhile, Haman had constructed a gallows on which he intended to have

Mordecai hung. During a sleepless night the king examined the court records and discovered that Mordecai had been given no reward for saving his life on one occasion.

When Haman came to the king to speak to him about hanging Mordecai, the king asked him what should be done for the man the king delighted to honor. Haman, thinking the king intended to honor him, suggested a number of honors and riches. The king then instructed Haman to do these things for Mordecai. When the king and Haman later went to the banquet prepared by Queen Esther, she spoke to the king about the threat to the Jewish people. When King Xerxes asked who was responsible for this threat, Esther replied that it was Haman. The king then instructed that Haman be hung on the gallows he had prepared for Mordecai.

Throughout the story of Esther, God's providence is evident. He brought Esther to the position of queen and saw that Mordecai was honored. He used Esther to protect his people. God preserved the lives of the Jews. He concurred in the actions of Haman, Mordecai, and Esther. He directed all things so that his purposes were served. He used government officials to rescue his people. God concurred in evil but made it serve a good purpose. The book of Esther clearly teaches that God cares for his people, but the actions of Mordecai and Esther teach that we need to care too; that we have a responsibility to see to the protection and the safety of others; that we need to use our minds, talents, abilities, positions, and opportunities to see to the welfare and the well-being of others and ourselves.

### The "eyes of the LORD"

The Bible is full of the doctrine of providence because God wants us to know how much and to what extent he cares for us in our daily lives. The book of Proverbs says, "The eyes of the LORD are everywhere, keeping watch on the wicked and the good" (15:3). God sees everything that happens; he knows everything that happens.

Concerning the land the Israelites were about to enter, Moses said, "It is a land the LORD your God cares for; the eyes of the LORD your God are continually on it from the beginning of the year to its end" (Deuteronomy 11:12). God cares for his world and everything in it. He never takes his eyes off it. What a comfort that is!

At one time the prophet Hanani came to King Asa of Judah and said, "The eyes of the LORD range throughout the earth to strengthen those whose hearts are fully committed to him" (2 Chronicles 16:9). The Lord doesn't miss anything that happens. What a reassurance that is for us today!

Psalm 139 is filled with insights regarding God's providence. There David says: "You have searched me and you know me. You know when I sit and when I rise; you perceive my thoughts from afar. You discern my going out and my lying down; you are familiar with all my ways. If I go up to the heavens, you are there; if I make my bed in the depths, you are there. If I rise on the wings of the dawn, if I settle on the far side of the sea, even there your hand will guide me, your right hand will hold me fast" (verses 1-3,8-10). David says the Lord even created his inmost being and knit him together in his mother's womb. He says that the Lord's eyes saw his unformed body. David realizes the Lord is so in control that he can say, "All the days ordained for me were written in your book before one of them came to be" (verse 16). How comforting that is!

The Bible gives us additional comfort by assuring us that Jesus, our blessed Savior, who came to this earth to live and die for us, is the one under whose feet God has placed all things and who is "appointed . . . to be head over everything for the church" (Ephesians 1:22). Jesus is preserving everything. Jesus is directing everything. Jesus is watching over everything and making everything serve a good purpose for us, his church of believers. What is there to fear? What can possibly go wrong? Jesus is in control.

The doctrine of providence is a very comforting doctrine and is thus a much-needed doctrine in our day and age. It's no secret that we live in an age of materialism and success orientation. Collecting things, buying things, getting things, being successful, getting ahead, being happy, trying to guarantee a comfortable retirement—these are what drive the world in which we live. How easy it is to be caught up by it all! It is also easy to experience the insecurities, pressures, and worries that accompany this kind of thinking. But if my happiness depends on what I own and what I achieve, I can never really be happy.

The doctrine of providence directs my attention elsewhere—to God and his concern for me. I don't have to worry about my life, about what I will eat or drink or what I will wear. If God takes care of the birds of the air, he surely will take care of me. Worrying cannot add a single hour to my life. If God takes care of the grass and the flowers, he will also take care of me. Why should I worry? My heavenly Father knows that I need all these things, and so I can seek his kingdom and his righteousness first with the confidence that everything I need for this life will be provided. I don't need to worry about tomorrow because God is going to take care of me tomorrow and the next day and the next day (Matthew 6:25-34). Yes, God cares for me.

And God cares for you too.

# Endnotes

[1]Francis Pieper, *Christian Dogmatics*, Vol. 1 (St. Louis: Concordia Publishing House, 1950), p. 485.

[2]Martin Luther, *What Luther Says: An Anthology*, compiled by Ewald M. Plass, 3 vols. (St. Louis: Concordia Publishing House, 1959), p. 1543.

[3]*What Luther Says*, p. 1543.

# For Further Reading

Bartels, Ernest. "A Lutheran Understanding of the Will and Providence of God," *Lutheran Synod Quarterly*, Vol. 32, No. 4 (December 1982); Vol. 33, No. 2 (June 1983); Vol. 33, No. 3 (September 1983).

Bente, Paul. "The Providence of God," in *The Abiding Word*, Vol. 2. St. Louis: Concordia Publishing House, 1947.

Hoenecke, Roland. "The Doctrine of Divine Providence," in *Our Great Heritage*, Vol. 2. Milwaukee: Northwestern Publishing House, 1991.

Pieper, Francis. *Christian Dogmatics*. Vol. 1. St. Louis: Concordia Publishing House, 1950.

Preus, Robert D. *The Theology of Post-Reformation Lutheranism*. Vol. 2. St. Louis: Concordia Publishing House, 1972.

Walther, C. F. W. *Convention Essays*. St. Louis: Concordia Publishing House, 1981.

# Scripture Index

# Subject Index